Simple Fruit Growing

OTHER CONCORDE GARDENING BOOKS

Simple
Fruit Growing

Roy Genders

WARD LOCK LIMITED · LONDON

© WARD LOCK LIMITED 1976

Laminated Paperboards ISBN 0 7063 5155 X
Paperback ISBN 0 7063 5157 6

First published in Great Britain 1976
by Ward Lock Limited, 116 Baker Street,
London, W1M 2BB

Text filmset in Times Roman (327)

Printed Offset Litho and bound by
Cox & Wyman Ltd,
London, Fakenham and Reading

Contents

1 The Fruit Garden

ITS PLANNING AND PLANTING

Most people love fruit, especially if it is fresh from the garden and, now more than ever, owing to its high cost in the shops, more and more people are taking a serious interest in growing their own. The high overheads that face the commercial grower make it necessary for him to grow only those varieties which crop heavily, so that many of those fruits of outstanding flavour which do not crop so heavily as others are largely neglected by commercial growers. All too often if you want to have something out of the ordinary, not often found in shops, you must grow it yourself.

If you have only a small garden you should grow only those fruits of compact habit. Indeed, there are several apples and pears, normally thought of as fairly large trees, which crop heavily when grown in large pots or tubs. A selection of these may be grown on a terrace or verandah, or around the walls of a small courtyard to provide an all year round supply of fruit. Among apples, the best for pots or tubs are:

'Lady Sudeley'	to mature in August
'Ellison's Orange'	to mature in September
'Egremont Russet'	to mature in October
'Sunset'	to mature in November
'Adam's Pearmain'	to mature in December
'Claygate Pearmain'	to mature January–March
'May Queen'	to mature April–June

All are spur bearing (of which more later), forming their fruits on short spurs and so maintaining a compact habit for many years. The one exception is 'Lady Sudeley', the best of all apples for pot and tub culture, which bears its fruit on short twigs or shoots and so is intermediate between the tip and spur bearing varieties. Among pears the following will provide fruit from pots or tubs over a long period:

'Laxton's Superb'	to mature in August
'Gorham'	to mature in September
'Conference'	to mature in October
'Louise Bonne'	to mature in November
'Glous Morceau'	to mature in December
'Winter Nelis'	to mature in January
'Santa Claus'	to mature in February

Pears may also be grown against a sunny wall in espalier form, as horizontal arms which grow out from each side of the main stem, one above the other, each being spaced about 16 in ≏ 40 cm apart. Pears like warmth and should be given the best place in the garden, where the fruit will receive the maximum amount of sunshine to ripen to perfection.

TYPES OF FRUIT TREE
Dessert plums should be given a similar position, especially those of greengage parentage which make the most delicious eating of all fruits when removed from the tree at the peak of perfection. Apples are hardier and so are grown in less select places. They may be grown as cordons (single stems) for which purpose the tip bearers are not suitable and 'Worcester Pearmain' is the best example, planted 3 ft ≏ 1 m apart alongside a path or to divide one part of the garden from another, training the stems against strong stakes fastened to galvanized wires. They come quickly into fruit as do those apples grown in dwarf pyramid form—a form which is also suitable for a small garden since they will produce a larger amount of fruit for the amount of ground they occupy than in any other form.

Standard trees are for the larger garden since they not only take up more space but also take longer to come into fruit, though when established they will bear heavily over a great many years. Several standards, perhaps four, could be planted down one side of the garden as ornamental trees, for there is

8

no livelier sight than the pink and white blossom in early summer as well as the bonus of the fruit. Of outstanding beauty when in bloom is 'Arthur Turner', a fine culinary apple and an excellent pollinator for 'Bramley's Seedling', which comes earlier into bearing and makes a sizeable fruit by mid-July. Also outstanding in bloom is 'Annie Elizabeth', the best of all long keeping cookers and, whilst flowering late, it is a valuable apple for frost-troubled gardens. Likewise the latest of all apples to bloom, 'Crawley Beauty', is a long-keeping dual purpose apple of quality.

Pears come earlier into bloom and plums earlier still. Pear blossom is white against which the dark brown anthers are conspicuous. Besides their blossom and beauty of fruit, they are handsome in leaf, the foliage of that excellent variety

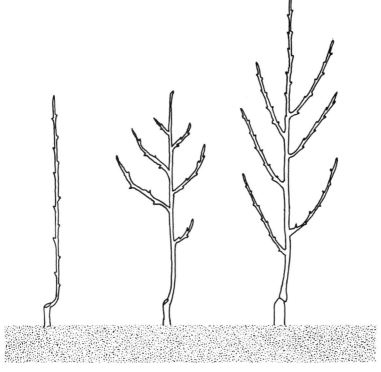

Types of fruit trees as usually purchased. *Left* a maiden, *centre* a feathered maiden, and *right* a two-year whip growth.

'Beurré Hardy' turning brilliant scarlet in autumn; that of 'Josephine de Malines' vivid yellow.

Cherries are rarely planted in small gardens as they crop well only as standards, and are difficult to pollinate whilst they take ten years to bear heavily.

CLIMATIC CONDITIONS

Climate is an important consideration when planning the fruit garden. Apples do better in the north than either plums or pears but there are varieties which bear well in cooler districts and those which prefer warmer areas. Some require the drier eastern side of Britain; others the moister atmosphere of the west. Those apples enjoying a cool dry climate are 'James Grieve' (the best pollinator for 'Cox's Orange'), 'Newton Wonder', 'Lord Derby', 'Miller's Seedling' and 'Bramley's Seedling', whilst in a moister climate plant 'Grenadier', 'Laxton's Superb', 'Cox's Orange Pippin' and 'Golden Delicious'. These four apples crop better south of a line drawn from Chester to the Wash and are grown in Cambridgeshire, Kent and Somerset on a commercial scale to supply the chief wholesale markets.

Pears require similar conditions to the more choice apples but even so, although the English apple stands comparison with any in the world, rarely does the English pear unless the summer and autumn is dry and warm for its ripening. In Britain, 'Jargonelle', 'Beurré Hardy' and 'Durondeau' will crop quite well at almost 1,000 ft $\simeq$ 330 m above sea level whilst 'Conference', 'Dr Jules Guyot', 'Laxton's Superb' and 'William's Bon Cretien' require a more sheltered garden and 'Roosevelt' and 'Doyenne du Comice' even greater warmth to crop and ripen well.

For cold windswept gardens, 'Winston' is an apple which usually does well and if its fruits were larger it would have been more widely planted commercially. Damsons also do well and may be planted as a windbreak or as a hedge, planting them in a double row 4 ft $\simeq$ 1·25 m apart and allowing 6 ft $\simeq$ 2 m between the trees in the rows. They are handsome in blossom and crop heavily most years. The Myrobalan or Cherry plum may be used in the same way.

For a cold north wall, the Myrobalan may be grown in the

fan-trained form, the method used for all the stone fruits, including the peach. Being so hardy, the Myrobalan will crop where no other fruit will grow and may be used to cover a courtyard or outhouse wall facing north. Or plant gooseberries as cordons, for this is another fruit enjoying cool conditions.

FRUITS FOR SUCCESSION

Strawberries can be planted beneath gooseberries for they appreciate the shelter from cold winds when in blossom and do well in dappled shade. If gooseberries are planted 5 ft $\simeq$ 1·6 m apart, in and between the rows, there will be room for a double row of strawberries in between and for early crops, these may be covered with barn cloches or with a continuous cloche made of p.v.c. sheeting stretched over hoops. The gooseberry is the first of the fruits to crop and amongst the first to mature are 'Whitesmith' and 'May Duke', the latter so good for culinary use. Then follows the first of the strawberries, 'Cambridge Early Pine' and 'Cambridge Regent', the latter the best early strawberry for a frost troubled garden for its blossom is highly resistant to frost from which the early strawberries tend to suffer. Both bear well in light soils as does 'Cambridge Favourite' which is also resistant to frost. It follows the other two and shortly after, comes 'Cambridge Rival' and the older 'Royal Sovereign', these two being the most delicious of all varieties. They prefer a heavy loam and should be grown away from a frost hollow. 'Cambridge Late Pine' and 'Talisman' conclude the summer season but in autumn there is 'Hampshire Maid', the German variety 'Gento' and the two famous French strawberries, 'La Sans Rivale' and 'Triomphe'. If covered with cloches they will continue fruiting until Christmas. There is also the upright growing strawberry, 'Sojana' which will reach a height of 6 ft $\simeq$ 2 m against a trellis or wall when the long runners may be tied in to wire or canes. Where there is no soil, it may be grown in pots in this way whilst the ordinary varieties may be grown in tubs or barrels drilled with holes and filled with soil. They will crop well in a courtyard or placed on a terrace or verandah.

As the summer strawberries are ending, the raspberry

Strawberry 'Royal Sovereign' ready for picking.

begins to crop. It has a much shorter season than the straw-berry though there are varieties which continue cropping until autumn and, for the amount of ground the plant occupies, it bears more heavily than any fruit. It requires a soil retentive of moisture and unlike the strawberry which will crop well on light land, it does well only in a heavy loam. In this respect it is like the black currant which enjoys entirely opposite conditions to the gooseberry both as to soil and climate. Black currants require a mild climate and, whereas gooseberries like dry conditions, currants prefer a moister atmosphere, hence the largest plantations are found in the west country and in Worcester and Hereford. Where rasp-berries fruit only on the new season's wood (except for the autumn fruiting varieties), black currants fruit both on the old and new wood so that the plants require large amounts of nitrogen to enable them to form a continual supply of new wood. If planted 5 ft $\simeq$ 1·6 m apart each way, strawberries may be grown in rows between them so as to make the best use of the land but raspberries are best grown in rows by themselves on one side of the fruit garden, possibly planting a dozen canes of each of five or six varieties to extend the season.

'Malling Exploit' is the first raspberry to ripen, the fruit being of excellent quality, but where frosts are troublesome grow instead 'Malling Jewel', for the blossom opens later and so is less likely to be ruined by frost and hence more reliable in its cropping. To follow are the new, heavy-cropping 'Glen Clova' and 'Malling Enterprise'—a seedling sister to 'Malling Jewel' and equally good. Then comes 'Norfolk Giant', still the best for freezing and canning. For September is the variety of that name and to continue the season into October and November, there is the Swiss introduction, 'Zeva'. Thus, with raspberries and strawberries, it is now possible to enjoy five months of fruiting so that if the early crops are caught by frost or spoiled by rain, this will not be the finish for that season as was the case in earlier years.

Fruiting in late July and August, the loganberry resembles the raspberry in that it fruits only on the new canes, the old ones being cut out after fruiting. The youngberry also fruits at this time. It is similar to the loganberry in that its long fruits do not part from the plug when gathered but for this reason are excellent for freezing and canning. To follow in September and early October is the thornless blackberry, 'Oregon', with its handsome fern-like foliage which should be planted against a trellis or rustic work used to make a cordon. Yields of 10–12 lbs of fruit from a single plant are not uncommon. In fruit at the same time is the vigorous 'Himalaya Giant' which bears enormous crops on both the old and new wood.

Here is a list of reliable soft fruits to provide a long season of picking. Size of garden and ground available will determine how many of each and how many varieties can be planted.

Fruit	Variety	Distance Apart	Season
Blackberry	'Bedford Giant'	6 ft	July–Aug.
	'Himalaya Giant'	10 ft	Sept.–Oct.
	'Oregon Thornless'	6 ft	Sept.–Oct.
Black currant	'Laxton's Giant'	5 ft	Late June
	'Mendip Cross'	5 ft	Early July
	'Wellington XXX'	5 ft	Mid-July
	'Westwick Triumph'	5 ft	Late July
	'Cotswold Cross'	5 ft	August
	'Amos Black'	5 ft	September
Gooseberry	'May Duke'	4 ft	Late May
	'Whitesmith'	4 ft	Early June
	'Keepsake'	4 ft	Early June
	'Dan's Mistake'	4 ft	Mid-June
	'Careless'	4 ft	Mid-June
	'Broom Girl'	4 ft	Late June
	'White Lion'	4 ft	Early July

Fruit	Variety	Distance Apart	Season
	'Gunner'	4 ft	Early July
	'Leveller'	4 ft	Early July
	'Howard's Lancer'	4 ft	Mid-July
Loganberry	'Thornless'	5 ft	July–Aug.
Raspberry	'Malling Jewel'	16 ins	July
	'Malling Exploit'	16 ins	July
	'Lloyd George'	16 ins	July
	'Glen Clova'	16 ins	Early Aug.
	'Malling Notable'	16 ins	Mid-Aug.
	'Norfolk Giant'	16 ins	Late Aug.
	'September'	16 ins	September
Red currant	'Laxton's No. 1.'	4 ft	Early Aug.
	'Red Lake'	3 ft	Mid-Aug.
Strawberry	'Cambridge Early Pine'	15 ins	Early June
	'Cambridge Premier'	15 ins	Early June
	'Cambridge Favourite'	15 ins	Mid-June
	'Cambridge Sentry'	15 ins	Late June
	'Royal Sovereign'	15 ins	Late June
	'Talisman'	15 ins	Early July
	'Cambridge Rearguard'	15 ins	Late July
	'Hampshire Maid'	15 ins	August
	'La Sans Rivale'	15 ins	September
	'Gento'	15 ins	Oct.–Nov.
Youngberry		6 ft	Aug.–Sept.

Do not plant soft fruits too close together, simply because they are small when received from the nursery. Gooseberries and black currants especially, soon spread out to form bushes 6 ft ≃ 2 m across. Allow them room to develop and until they have grown large, plant strawberries (or vegetables) between the rows.

SOIL REQUIREMENTS

Most fruits are accommodating as to soil and although raspberries and black currants prefer a heavy soil, they will crop well in a light soil which contains plenty of humus. Most soft fruits require a humus-laden soil, though apart from blackberries and black currants, they do not require large amounts of manure. These two fruits do, because they fruit both on the old and new wood and bearing fruit and new wood at the same time, require plenty of nourishment. Soft fruits also need humus to conserve moisture in summer for it is during the drier months that they fruit. So incorporate plenty of humus-forming materials before planting. Use clearings from ditches; material from the compost heap; peat; decayed leaves and lawn mowings; cotton or wool shoddy; farmyard manure; or used hops, usually obtainable from a brewery for a small sum. Shoddy, hops and farmyard manure have the advantage over other forms of humus in that they contain the nitrogen so essential for the plants to make new growth and it is slowly released over a long period. Other forms of organic nitrogenous manures are bone meal, poultry manure and fish meal which should be used with those humus-forming materials which contain little plant food. If you live near the coast you will find that chopped seaweed has a similar nitrogen and potash content to poultry manure. Gooseberries and strawberries are lovers of potash and this may be supplied as wood and bonfire ash which has been stored dry so that the potash content will not have been washed away. Potash is also present in fish meal and poultry manure. Farmyard manure contains only a trace of potash and shoddy and used hops none at all and, where used, it is advisable to rake into the soil before planting strawberries and gooseberries, and in spring each year afterwards, a 1 oz per sq. yd dressing of sulphate of potash, an inorganic fertilizer with 50 per cent potash content.

16

Strawberry 'Cambridge Favourite', one of the most widely planted and reliable varieties

It is sometimes necessary to thin gooseberries when fruit of a uniform size is required

Use it with care as it is expensive, and apply it to the surface for the rains to wash in.

All fruits require a deeply worked soil for they mostly send down their roots to a great depth in search of food and moisture, so work in the humus and plant foods to a depth of two spits (spades) at least. The time to do this is in autumn. Then leave the ground in a rough state when the soil will be pulverized by wind and rain and hard frosts.

After forking over the ground or double digging it, working in the humus materials as the task proceeds, give it a liberal dressing on the surface with hydrated lime which will be washed in during winter. But if the soil is heavy and sticky, apply to it as the digging proceeds, a dr..ring of unhydrated (caustic) lime which, when in contact with moisture in the soil, disintegrates in a violent reaction, causing the soil particles to be broken up. It will leave even a heavy soil in a friable condition. In heavy soils, work in peat and any kind of grit or shingle.

At the same time, treat the soil for wireworms for no pest is more destructive to strawberries and most other soft fruits. Gamma-BHC powder should be sprinkled into the soil as it is turned over but where used do not plant potatoes in the same ground for at least twelve months afterwards. A crop of potatoes is excellent for cleaning weed infested ground before planting fruit and it is imperative to clear the ground thoroughly at this time as it is almost impossible to do so after planting when the plants become an entangled mass of weeds which eventually chokes them to death. Planting in clean, well nourished ground is the first essential in fruit growing.

Land that is of a shallow nature, with no more than 2–3 in $\backsimeq$ 5–7 cm of top soil overlying a chalky subsoil, may be brought into more suitable condition by 'green' manuring. The method is to sow rape seed thickly over the surface. This is done in late summer so that it quickly germinates and it is dug as deeply as possible into the soil when about 3 in $\backsimeq$ 7·5 cm tall. Both the 'green' top and the mass of fibrous roots will add valuable humus and increase the depth of soil. If the surface is dressed with peat before digging, this will be of additional value. Then add whatever manures are available.

Neither greenhouse nor frame nor propagator are necessary

for fruit growing. Strawberries are increased by runners and raspberries by the formation of new canes each year. Gooseberries and black currants are readily propagated from cuttings rooted in trenches of sandy soil. Most fruit crops are of a permanent nature and, once planted, all that is necessary to keep them healthy is the judicious removal of dead wood.

The use of cloches will however, extend the strawberry season. The earliest varieties such as 'Cambridge Premier' and 'Profusion' may be covered with barn-type cloches early in May when the fruit will be ripe by the month end and the Remontant or autumn-fruiting varieties such as 'La Sans Rivale' will ripen their fruit until Christmas in the south if covered with cloches in late October. Do not cover those varieties susceptible to mildew such as 'Cambridge Regent', the best early variety for northern gardens as its blossom is resistant to frosts. Under cloches it rarely does well.

Vines may also be grown under cloches, training the shoots formed just above soil level in opposite directions, covering them during the latter weeks of summer and early autumn whilst the grapes are ripening and before the cloches are used to cover late strawberries.

FREEZING

Many soft fruits are excellent for freezing and each year, new varieties are introduced specially for the purpose. It is essential for them to retain their shape and eating qualities after they have been frozen for twelve months and some older varieties do not do this. The deep freeze is most valuable for those fruits which are produced during 'glut' periods, so that none need be wasted. They must however, be frozen when in the peak of condition.

Fruits required for deep freezing should be picked just before they are fully ripe. To allow them to become over-ripe will mean they will become 'mushy' before they are frozen. Gooseberries present no problem but blackberries, strawberries and raspberries should be placed individually on trays so that the fruits do not touch each other and then placed in the deep freezer for 2 hours to become partially frozen and so that they retain their shape when removed from the freezer. They are then placed in the cellophane bags and put back in the freezer with the minimum delay where they will keep at least a year in perfect condition. They will need 2–3 hours to thaw before using.

Some fruits freeze better than others. In strawberries, omit those which ripen to a deep crimson and are excessively sweet such as 'Cambridge Aristocrat' and 'Rearguard'. Grow them for eating straight from the plant, but for freezing grow 'Royal Sovereign', 'Cambridge Vigour' and 'Favourite'. Among raspberries, 'Malling Jewel', 'Lloyd George', 'Glen Clova' and 'Norfolk Giant' freeze well. Among black currants, 'Mendip Cross', 'Cotswold Cross' and 'Wellington XXX' are excellent, the fruits having thicker than average skins. Loganberries and youngberries freeze well since they have a core. Among blackberries, 'Himalaya Giant' and 'Oregon Thornless', retain their shape and quality after picking and freeze extremely well.

2 Strawberries

To quote Isaac Walton: 'Indeed we may say of angling as Dr. Boteler said of strawberries: "Doubtless God could have made a better berry but doubtless God never did".' But in Walton's day, it was the wild strawberries that were so much enjoyed in June. They were small but sweet and juicy though they had but a short season. Today, there are varieties to extend the growing season from mid-May (under cloches) until Christmas in the more favourable districts, covering the plants with cloches in late October. Where no cloches are available, strawberries may be enjoyed from early June in the south, until the end of October, thus giving a greatly extended season compared with pre-war days when they cropped only in June in the south, July in the north, and adverse weather could spoil the entire crop. Of all soft fruits grown today, the area given over to strawberries amounts to half the total but most is given to those which freeze and can well.

SOIL REQUIREMENTS

Strawberries prefer a light, well drained soil, fenland soil or one of a sandy nature especially and of all fruits, their blossom is most prone to frost damage. For low-lying land where late frosts persist, plant only the resistant varieties for early crops. These are 'Cambridge Early Pine', 'Cambridge Regent' and 'Cambridge Vigour', the latter being the best early variety to plant in a limestone soil which will rarely grow good crops. Nor are strawberries a reliable crop in excessively wet areas for the soft fruit, held just above soil level is often spoilt by soil splashing, and decays with too much moisture.

The best varieties for areas of high rainfall are 'Cambridge Favourite' and 'Rival', both of which hold their glossy-skinned fruits well above the foliage making ripening (and picking) easier in a sunless summer, besides the fruits being well above the soil. But whereas the strawberry must be removed as soon as ripe, whatever the weather, the gooseberry and black currant may be left on the plants until conditions are more suitable for their picking. Again, strawberries are difficult to keep clean of weeds for they have a creeping matted habit and it is no use planting them in dirty land.

A light soil will warm more quickly in spring and the plants will be stimulated into growth sooner than where growing in heavy soil. Also, it will not become too consolidated whilst the fruit is being picked. Again, light land will be well drained in winter and this will eliminate the risk of red core root rot which gives the plants a stunted appearance and greatly reduces their cropping before they die back altogether.

If the soil is not too well drained, work in some shingle and peat and when digging the ground, incorporate plenty of compost, decayed leaves and lawn mowings, also straw which has been composted with an activator. Varieties resistant to red core should always be planted in heavy soil and these include most of the Cambridge varieties such as 'Premier', 'Rival' and 'Vigour' for early crops; 'Red Gauntlet' and 'Talisman' for later. They should also be planted a month earlier than where growing in light land, to become well established before winter.

Strawberries require a balanced diet, as they take from the soil nitrogen, phosphorus and potash in equal amounts. Farmyard manure contains each of these foods, as does straw composted with an activator and to which some poultry manure has been added. If shoddy is used, augment it by steamed bone flour and sulphate of potash, giving 1 oz per sq. yd of each. Remember that the lighter the soil the more potash will be required. These fertilizers are raked into the surface before planting.

Strawberries also crop best in a slightly acid soil so that peat can be used generously, but though it provides valuable humus it contains no plant food. It should therefore be used with farmyard manure or poultry manure, or with those plant foods previously described. Plenty of humus and plant food is the secret of success with strawberries and the land must be in good 'heart' at planting time. Strawberries do well following a crop of potatoes which will leave the soil in a fine tilth.

A big advantage the strawberry has over other fruits is that it will crop heavily within nine months of planting, that is if the soil has been well prepared. Gardeners of old would plant in October and disbud the first year, to build up a strong plant to crop heavily the following year but this is not necessary. If planting of the early varieties is done in September, whilst the soil is still warm and those which fruit later are planted in October, there will be good crops the following summer. Then, if the plants are kept free of runners, they will conserve their energies, making large plants to bear double the amount of fruit the following year.

PLANTING

If the soil is heavy and the land not too well drained, it will be advisable to plant in raised beds made 4–5 ft $\simeq$ 1·25–1·5 m wide so that picking the fruit may be done from either side without treading the beds. Three rows are planted, allowing about 2 ft $\simeq$ 60 cm between the rows and spacing the plants 15 in $\simeq$ 40 cm in the rows.

In a light loam, plant on the flat, giving the same spacing, but if planting between rows of gooseberries, plant a double row 15 in $\simeq$ 40 cm apart and allow 18 in $\simeq$ 50 cm in the rows. Too close planting will encourage mildew, especially in the west where a more humid atmosphere prevails. Where using barn cloches this spacing will also be suitable.

Those plants in rows should be kept free of runners for the first two years after planting. They may be allowed to form runners the next year and these are removed in September and a new plantation made, the old plants being destroyed for strawberries will only crop well for about three years after which new plantings should be made in fresh ground.

Plants in raised beds are allowed to form runners which will fruit the following year and the beds are left down for two or three years before being removed. It is not advisable to plant in beds those varieties which make plenty of leaf for fear of an outbreak of mildew which may happen if the plants are too close together. An exception is 'Cambridge Early Pine' which, though making plenty of leaf, is resistant to mildew.

Where grown in beds, strawberries are little troubled by frost, they seem to protect each other. Nor do they suffer from drought for the foliage shields the roots from the direct rays of the sun. There is also little loss of fruit through soil splashing and plants in beds do not need strawing as those in rows do.

When planting strawberries, purchase 'runners' which are from one-year plants. 'Maidens' they are called and the most vigorous are those which have formed first, those which are nearest the parent plant. They are detached with scissors or pruners and should be planted without delay. If one has room, several one-year plants should be kept for this purpose and not allowed to form fruit. Half a dozen plants will give about fifty runners which will have rooted around the parent plants but which are readily pulled up.

Always purchase the original stock from a grower who guarantees 'Certified Plants'. This means that they have been inspected by an official of the Ministry of Agriculture and certified as virus-free stock. If sent any distance, they will be wrapped in cellophane with the roots in damp moss for the runners must not be allowed to dry out. The roots must be kept moist so that the plants will get away to a good start. This is especially important where planting early fruiting varieties.

If planting early in autumn, the soil will usually be in a friable condition but never plant into wet, sticky ground, nor when there is frost in the soil. Use a blunt-nosed trowel for planting and make the rows running north to south to ensure the even ripening of the fruit. Spread out the fibrous roots; plants will never do well if the roots are bunched together, but do not plant too deeply. Like most soft fruits, strawberries are surface rooting and never do well if planted deeply: hence they may be grown in shallow soils and will crop well there if top dressed. Use a garden line for planting for it is important that the rows have the correct spacing, not only to allow the plants room to develop but for a hand or mechanical hoe to be taken between the rows to suppress weeds and without going too close to the plants.

Plant firmly, treading in the plants and if frost is experienced soon afterwards, it is advisable to go along the rows when the soil is friable again, to tread in any loosened plants. In a dry autumn, it will be advisable to water in the plants and to give further waterings until established.

BRINGING ON THE CROP

Early in spring, hoe between the plants to break up the surface soil to allow air and moisture to reach the roots and in April, if the spring is cold, give a light top dressing ($\frac{1}{2}$ oz per sq. yd) between the rows with sulphate of ammonia to stimulate the plants into growth. This should be applied on a showery day when it will be immediately washed into the soil.

By the end of April, under normal conditions, plants of early fruiting varieties will be forming blossom and a hard frost at this time may blacken the blossom and put paid to any crop that year. Frost resistant varieties may be only slightly damaged and those which bloom and fruit later will escape altogether. It is therefore advisable to plant a row of each of four or five varieties with different flowering and fruiting times so as to spread the risk.

Soon after the blossom has set, the plants are given a mulch. Peat or strawy manure spread thickly between the plants will help to conserve moisture in the soil and will also prevent soil splashing on to the fruit. The old growers put clean straw between the rows and right up to the plants which served the same purpose, hence the fruit took its name from this practise. If straw is used, put down a slug repellent or first water the ground with Slugit for the pests can devour a lot of fruit in a single night and make it most unsightly. Damp paper may also be used between the rows and mats made of bamboo or plastic, which are quite inexpensive. Whatever material is used, it must be in position before the fruits begin to ripen, which in the south will be during the first days of June; about two weeks later in the north. As soon as the fruit begins to swell, it will colour rapidly and the plants will need to be picked over at least once daily.

May and June is generally the driest part of the year and at this time, whilst the fruit is swelling, the plants may need additional supplies of moisture. In dry weather, unless the ground contains plenty of humus to hold moisture, the fruits

26

Tucking straw beneath strawberry trusses.

will not swell to any size and will ripen hard and seedy. It is therefore important to water them frequently and this is best done in the evening so that the moisture will penetrate to the roots during the night. When watering, always give the soil a thorough soaking.

27

When the fruit is beginning to turn red, watering is withheld for a day or two until the ripe fruit is removed. Then water again if the soil is dry. In this way the fruit will be dry when gathered and will freeze better, whilst the berries will keep their shape if used fresh.

The plants will also benefit from an occasional watering with dilute liquid manure, purchased in bottles as a proprietary make, or it may be made by immersing a sack half filled with manure, in a barrel or tank and leaving it for a week or two. After removal of the sack, fill up the tank with water and use as required.

After fruiting, clear the ground of straw if this has been used to keep the fruit clean, and burn it or compost it, to dig back later. If peat is used, it will soon become assimilated into the soil, improving the humus content and texture. As the foliage dies back in late autumn, it is best removed by going over the plants with shears, and burning it. The new foliage will grow from the crown of the plant the following spring. Then give the plants a 1 oz per sq. yd dressing of sulphate of potash in early March, followed by a similar application of sulphate of ammonia between the rows a month later. When the blossom appears, mulch between the rows and you will have an even bigger crop from the second-year plants.

When to remove the plants will depend upon their continued health and vigour. They should crop for at least three seasons, maybe four if you look after them.

Early fruit, from the beginning of May, can be enjoyed if the early varieties (or some of them) are covered with cloches. Glass barn type or continuous cloches of p.v.c. sheeting are suitable for both cover ground 2 ft $\simeq$ 60 cm in width so that the foliage is not crowded together, which would encourage mildew. For this reason, mildew-resistant varieties and those which do not make excess leaf should be planted for cloching. Only second- and third-year plants are covered and the cloches should not go over them until early March. Strawberries are hardy plants and require the winter months to get a good soaking and recover from their heavy cropping of the previous summer. Give the plants a teaspoonful of sulphate of potash each before the cloches are placed over them. It is also advisable to dust the new foliage which will now be appearing with flowers of sulphur to prevent mildew and if the soil is dry, give it a soaking around the plants. By mid-March, the sun will be increasing in strength and the plants will need ventilation on warm days. This is done by raising a cloche or two along the row to allow more air to enter during daytime. The cloche should be in place again before evening. But in March, the plants will appreciate being protected from the cold winds which blow.

By April 1st, the cloches are left off on all warm days and the plants will benefit from the showery weather at this time. They will soon be in bloom and to uncover the plants on suitable days will help with their fertilization. If cold winds prevail, keep the plants covered: also cover after the fruit begins to set, removing the cloches only to water for the plants now require plenty of moisture to help the fruits to swell. Take care not to splash soil on to the fruits and foliage. Replace the cloches as soon as surplus moisture has dried off the foliage. By May 1st the first fruits will be ready to pick and it will be advisable to look over the plants every other day, removing the cloches only to pick the fruit and to water. When cropping finishes, remove the cloches and mulch the plants heavily whilst keeping them well watered through summer.

AUTUMN-FRUITING STRAWBERRIES
Cloches are also used to cover the Remontant or autumn-fruiting strawberries. These have been grown in France for years but are only now becoming known in Britain. They may be planted as late as early April, for the blossom is removed until the end of June, during which time a large plant is formed. Mulch and feed the plants in the same way as for the ordinary varieties. In a dry, sunny autumn they will ripen large quantities of fruit even without cloching but cloches are necessary to continue the cropping from November 1st until Christmas. They do especially well in the south.

The method of growing is to plant a double row 18 in ≃ 46 cm apart, which will permit them to be covered by a barn cloche. Space the plants 18 in ≃ 46 cm in the rows and allow them to form runners which will also bloom and fruit in autumn by which time the beds will have become a mass of plants all bearing fruit. The soil must be well prepared before planting otherwise the fruit will be small. Keep the plants well watered throughout summer and from early July, give them a watering with liquid manure in alternate weeks to build up strong plants by the end of August when they begin to fruit. If the autumn is cold and wet, cover the plants early September but usually, mid-October is the best time and the plants are kept covered until Christmas. The flowers of several varieties are frost hardy and I have had 'La Sans Rivale' in fruit in pots on a sunny outside window sill on Christmas Day with the plants covered in hoar frost. These strawberries should be grown wherever late frosts are experienced which may prevent the early strawberries from fruiting. Usually autumn is a dry, sunny time of year and if other strawberries fail, the autumn varieties will compensate. It is excess moisture rather than cold which causes the fruit to decay, and it is botrytis that mostly troubles the autumn strawberries. Allow the cloches to remain open at each end of the row to allow a free circulation of air which will keep the plants and the fruit dry.

The plants die down completely after fruiting and early in spring when they begin to grow again, remove the older plants from the beds (they will no longer be in neat rows), allowing the runners, some of which have already fruited, to remain to fruit again. Those in turn will send out more runners which will fruit in autumn. It is necessary however, to feed the plants well during spring and summer, otherwise they will impoverish the soil and the fruit will be small and hard. Do them well and you will be rewarded a hundredfold. The fruit can be used fresh and it freezes well.

GROWING IN BARRELS AND TUBS
Strawberries may be grown in barrels and tubs into which holes of 1 in $\backsimeq$ 2·5 cm diameter are drilled and spaced 16 in $\backsimeq$ 40 cm apart. A small courtyard or verandah could take several tubs (barrels cut in half across the middle) which are obtainable from cider and vinegar makers. They are of oak and are long lasting. Planting is done in the holes around the tub, also at the top and if several are used, each may be planted with a separate variety to provide a succession of fruit through summer. 'Cambridge Premier' and 'Talisman' do well in tubs.

First place at the bottom of the tub, which must have drainage holes, a 3 in $\approx$ 7·6 cm layer of crushed bricks or crocks, then a layer of turves of similar thickness, grass side downwards. The tub is then filled up with fresh loam into which has been incorporated some moist peat and some decayed manure or used hops. Mix well together before adding a handful of bone meal and one of sulphate of potash, again mixing it well. After filling, allow the compost a week to settle and it will then be about 2 in $\approx$ 5 cm below the rim. This will allow for watering without the compost splashing over the edge.

Set the plants 6 in $\approx$ 15 cm apart at the top and use a length of wood to plant them in the compost where the holes are. Planting is done in autumn when several pickings of fruit will be enjoyed the following summer with larger amounts next year. Remember, never allow the plants, especially in the side holes, to lack moisture and when making new leaf in spring and setting the fruit, it may be necessary to give the tubs a soaking twice weekly but never so much as to percolate through the drainage holes.

The plants will respond to an occasional watering with dilute liquid manure after the fruit has set.

VARIETIES
Early
'CAMBRIDGE EARLY PINE' The first to ripen its fruit and, though making plenty of foliage, it shows a high resistance to mildew. The fruit is round and of a bright scarlet colour with a smooth glossy skin which allows moisture to drain away. The blossom is resistant to frost which makes it the best early variety for low-lying land.

'CAMBRIDGE PREMIER' Resistant to mildew and red core root rot, it ripens several days later than 'Early Pine' and is the best early for areas of high rainfall. The scarlet, wedge-shaped fruits freeze well and as it makes only a small amount of foliage, it cloches well.

'CAMBRIDGE REGENT' Shows marked resistance to frost, and is the heaviest cropper in all soils among the early varieties and is the best early for northern gardens. Susceptible to mildew, it is not one of the best for cloching.

31

'HÂTIVE DE CAEN' A hardy, frost-resistant variety grown in Holland in preference to other earlies. It makes a large leafy plant, the round fruits ripening to deep pink and possessing rich perfume.

Second Early

'CAMBRIDGE FAVOURITE' One of the most widely planted of varieties for it crops well in all soils and is rarely troubled by frost, drought or mildew. The best variety for a light, sandy soil, the large, red fruits freeze and travel well. It crops well over a very long season.

'CAMBRIDGE RIVAL' This prefers a heavy soil and the damp climate of the west country where it is now grown to the exclusion of most others. Bearing its fruit well above the foliage, it makes for easy picking and clean fruit, the conical berries being bright crimson and of exceptional flavour.

'CAMBRIDGE VIGOUR' A second early which at the East Malling trials recorded the heaviest crop, whilst the plants bear well when four years old. Resistant to red core, it crops well even in a limestone soil, the fruits ripening to deepest crimson.

Mid-Season

'CAMBRIDGE SENTRY' The best mid-season variety for areas of high rainfall, holding its fruit above the soil, cropping well in a heavy soil and showing resistance to mildew and botrytis. The wedge-shaped fruit retains its bright crimson colour after freezing and is sweet and juicy.

'RED GAUNTLET' A compact grower with small foliage, it holds its fruit well above the ground, the large scarlet fruits possessing excellent flavour whilst it crops well in all soils.

'ROYAL SOVEREIGN' For flavour and appearance, this has remained outstanding since its introduction in 1892. The large, scarlet, wedge-shaped fruits always take pride of place on the show bench. To crop heavily, it must be grown well. Always obtain the virus-free Malling 48 strain.

'SOUVENIR DE CHARLES MACHIROEX' In continental Europe this takes the place of our own 'Royal Sovereign', for it crops heavily, its large conical dark crimson fruits with red flesh possessing exceptional flavour.

32

Late

'CAMBRIDGE LATE PINE' As valuable a variety as 'Early Pine', cropping heavily, its large, round, crimson fruits being sugar-sweet whilst they freeze and bottle well.

'CAMBRIDGE REARGUARD' The latest of all the summer varieties, this crops well in all soils and especially in the drier eastern counties, the large, crimson, wedge-shaped fruits possessing a distinct sharp flavour.

'FENLAND WONDER' A plant was discovered growing on a churchyard wall in Norfolk in 1952 and it is now widely planted in East Anglia for the fruit is large, of excellent flavour and it crops heavily over a long season.

'MONTROSE' A new late variety, ripening the bulk of its fruit late in August, the round, orange fruits having pink flesh and a fresh acid flavour. It cloches well at this time.

'TALISMAN' This may be classed as late mid-season and it is a tremendous cropper but best grown in the drier parts of Britain for its conical fruit tends to be soft, though it freezes well if picked on the point of ripening.

Autumn-Fruiting

'GENTO' This ripens its berries in September and it maintains its size of fruit until it has finished cropping in October. The conical, light-red fruit is firm enough for freezing, with a pleasant, slightly acid, flavour.

'HAMPSHIRE MAID' This crops after 'Late Pine', being at its best in the latter part of August and into September when the Continental varieties take over. The large, round, conical fruits ripen to deep crimson but remain firm after freezing. It crops over a long season but needs a well nourished soil and plenty of water.

'LA SANS RIVALE' This begins to crop in late September and continues until the year ends, the conical fruit ripening to pale red: of good flavour. In a sunny autumn, each plant is capable of producing 2 lbs of fruit.

'ST CLAUDE' Crops over a longer season than any variety, forming its first fruits mid-August and continuing until Christmas. The conical fruits ripen to deep crimson and are sweet and of good flavour.

3 Raspberries

Raspberries are our chief provider of soft fruit after the main strawberry crop is over, possessing a unique flavour. The fruits freeze well and make excellent jam, though the advent of the freezer has meant that few people have any surplus fruit for preserving. As with the strawberry, there are now varieties which will spread the season over many weeks so that a period of wet weather, which may spoil the fruit of one variety, does not mean the destruction of the whole crop. As the canes grow upright, to about 5–6 ft $\approx$ 2 m above soil level, picking the fruit is easier than with strawberries and, once planted, if well looked after, a plantation will remain in bearing for many years, and no hardy plant bears more fruit for the amount of garden space it occupies.

Flowering later than the strawberry, most varieties of raspberry miss the late frosts, but the canes should be protected from cold winds if the garden is exposed. This may be done by erecting interwoven fencing around the fruit and vegetable garden or by planting a hedge of *Cupressus leylandii*, spacing the plants 2 ft $\approx$ 60 cm apart and in two years they will have reached a height of 5–6 ft $\approx$ 2 m. Strong winds blowing directly on to the raspberries may cause the canes to break, with a reduction in the following season's crop.

If the garden is in a frost hollow, it is advisable to reduce risk from frost damage to a minimum and to grow the later flowering varieties such as 'Malling Jewel', 'Glen Clova' and 'Norfolk Giant', which will fruit in that order, with 'September Abundance' and 'November Abundance' to provide fruit in autumn. Though 'Malling Jewel' blooms

34

Blackberry *Rubus fruticosus*, the wild blackberry

ABOVE Apple 'Cox's Orange Pippin'
LEFT Apple 'Worcester Pearmain'

early, it is frost resistant whereas 'Malling Promise', which blooms at the same time, is prone to frost damage and should really only be planted on high ground or near the coast.

Plant raspberries along one side or at one end of the fruit garden, preferably with the cane rows oriented north–south to ensure the even ripening of the fruit.

SOIL REQUIREMENTS

The raspberry enjoys a soil capable of retaining summer moisture, but also one which is well-drained in winter. A heavy loam is ideal and if the soil is light and sandy, incorporate plenty of humus in autumn before planting. Peat is valuable, to hold moisture in dry weather as is garden compost, whilst farmyard manure is best of all. Of all soft fruits, raspberries detest drought and will produce only weak, thin canes and small seedy fruit unless well supplied with moisture. Where humus is in short supply, compost some straw or bracken with an activator and add to it a small quantity of poultry manure. Shoddy is also valuable and chopped seaweed. To produce an abundance of new canes, the plants need plenty of nitrogen to stimulate new growth since short, weakly canes produce small seedy fruits and the plantation will soon die out. If plenty of humus cannot be obtained, raspberries should not be grown. Just before planting, rake in 1 oz of sulphate of potash per yard of row or use wood ash if it has been stored under cover. It is also important to plant in clean ground for it is impossible to do so later without disturbing the fibrous roots which grow out to a considerable distance. For this reason, do not cultivate too near the canes when hoeing between the rows.

Plant the canes early November before hard frosts are experienced. At that time, the soil will be still warm and friable and the canes will become established before winter. Planting can take place until March but not if the soil is wet or sticky after snow, or if there is frost in it. It will be better to dig a trench and 'heel in' the canes, covering the roots with straw or sacking with soil on top. They will take no harm here until conditions for planting are suitable. Always purchase Certified stock passed by the Ministry of Agriculture as being free from 'mosaic', a disease which will cause stunted canes.

Purchase the canes from a reliable source and remember that good stock will remain vigorous almost indefinitely if it is well looked after and the original cost will be the only one.

The canes are planted 16–18 in ≃ 46 cm apart in the rows, depending upon the vigour of the variety. 'Malling Promise' shows exceptional vigour and should be spaced 20 in ≃ 50 cm apart. It is a rule to allow the same distance between the rows as the plants grow tall. This is about 5 ft ≃ 2·75 m for most varieties and 6 ft ≃ 2 m for 'Malling Exploit', 'Promise' and 'Norfolk Giant'.

Take care with the planting since planting too deep is the most common cause of failure. Because the canes are long when received, it is thought that they must be put well into the ground so that they will better support themselves. This is wrong, for to plant deeper than 3 in ≃ 7·5 cm will cause the plants to make little new cane growth. The old gardeners would plant no more than 2 in ≃ 5 cm deep. The late George Pyne of Topsham, introducer of 'Pyne's Royal' and other good raspberries, advised planting at this depth, especially on heavy land. The same applies to loganberries and blackberries. In fact, of all soft fruits, only black currants like deep planting.

Make the canes firm by treading and after a few days, cut back to within 8 in ≃ 20 cm of soil level. This will mean that there will be no fruit the first season, apart from the autumn varieties which will fruit on the new canes formed during the summer after planting. This is one reason why summer raspberries are not so widely planted as strawberries, for one has to wait eighteen months for the first crop. Because of this, it is advisable to plant a dozen or so canes of the autumn varieties, but to get them well established first it is advisable to plant the canes in November.

CARE AFTER PLANTING

Early in spring, tread the plants again for they may have become loosened by hard frost and firm planting is important to the formation of new canes. Then, when the new canes are about 18 in ≃ 46 cm high, which will be early in June, the rows will need staking.

Strong stakes are driven well into the ground at intervals

of 8 ft ≃ 2·5 m to which galvanized wires are fastened about 15 in ≃ 36 cm above ground and at 15 in ≃ 36 cm intervals to the top. The stakes should be about 6 ft ≃ 2 m high and as the canes continue to grow all summer, tie them in to the top so that if winds are troublesome, the canes will not break. Space the canes out as evenly as possible and tie in with twine which is cut away when the old canes are cut out in autumn.

Another way of supporting the canes is known as the rope method. Here the canes are fastened together in arches, tied to stout stakes 6 ft ≃ 2 m high and at intervals of about 6 ft ≃ 2 m so that wires are not used. The canes are bent over in arches and tied to the stakes. This partly checks the flow of sap to the tops and makes for more even ripening of the fruit along the entire length of the canes. Both methods have their advantages and staking and tying is all important since badly staked plants result in damaged canes whilst making picking a more difficult task.

During summer, early June being a suitable time, the plants will benefit from a mulch of decayed manure or compost, augmented by some peat. This will help to conserve moisture in the soil and suppress weeds. It should be applied right up to the plants and to a depth of 3–4 in ≃ 8–10 cm. A mixture of partly composted lawn mowings and peat is excellent, for it readily works down into the soil during summer. In times of drought it may be necessary to water artificially to maintain cane growth and size of fruit when the canes are in bearing. Give the rows a good soaking, preferably in the evening and spray the foliage often to guard against red spider.

In November, after fruiting (and the canes produced one year will fruit the next year) the old canes are cut out to 1 in ≃ 2·5 cm above soil level. Too much cane should not be left as it will only encourage pests and disease. Burn the old canes and as they are removed, cut out any weakly new canes, leaving 6–8 strong ones to each 'stool', as raspberry roots are called. These will have been tied in during the summer and by late autumn, the rows will be neat and tidy and require no further attention until next June.

With autumn-fruiting varieties, the canes are left until early March and are cut back to 1 in ≃ 2·5 cm of soil level, for it is on the same year's canes that the fruit is borne. As these varieties have to produce new canes and bear fruit at the same time, they require heavy dressings of farmyard or poultry manure, augmented by peat and lawn mowings given in June and again in August.

Raspberries are gathered just before the fruit is fully ripe, whilst the berries are firm but not hard and in no way 'mushy'. If over-ripe they will be difficult to pick as they part from the core and are easily crushed. They should be red but not crimson. If covered with sugar and placed in a refrigerator for several hours they will be in perfect condition to serve with cream or after sprinkling with red wine. The fruits will continue to ripen after picking. It is not advisable to pick the fruit if covered with moisture during rainy weather. First allow them an hour or so to dry off.

To propagate raspberries, lift a root or two in November and pull off the new canes with their fibrous roots, 'teazing' them away from the old 'stool'. Any weak or stunted canes are discarded. It is not advisable to replant in ground which has been growing raspberries before. Select a fresh place and after planting as described, cut back the canes to allow the plants to form new canes the following summer.

A word of warning. When lifting the roots for propagation, and the same may be said where planting canes purchased from a grower, never allow the roots to dry out for if they do, the plants will rarely recover. Plant or 'heel in' at once or place them in a cool room with the roots in deep boxes covered with soil, until such time as they can be planted.

VARIETIES
Early

'LLOYD GEORGE' Introduced in 1920 and for many years the only variety for early fruit. Gradually it lost vigour and only the introduction of virus-free, New Zealand stocks after the war brought about its revival. For flavour it has no equal, whilst it bears heavy crops of bright red fruits in all soils.

'MALLING EXPLOIT' A fine early variety, bearing heavy crops of large scarlet berries of great firmness which retain their colour and quality after picking. It is one of the best for freezing. Cane growth is vigorous and spreading.

'MALLING PROMISE' The first of the late Mr Norman

Grubb's introductions from East Malling which revolution-
ized raspberry growing after the war. It is the first to ripen its
fruit but is more liable to frost damage than others, whilst
its tall canes may also be harmed by hard frosts in winter.
Best grown in the warmer parts of Britain where it has no
peer, being resistant to virus and propagating well.

'ROYAL SCOT' One of the earliest varieties, the fruits
ripening to deep salmon-pink with exceptional flavour and
borne evenly along the branches, which makes for easy
picking. The fruits 'plug' well and retain their shape and
firmness in wet weather.

Mid-Season

'GLEN CLOVA' A new Scottish variety of merit, flowering
late and so escaping the frosts. It bears large crops of bright
red fruits which are sweet and juicy and retain their qualities
after freezing.

'MALLING ENTERPRISE' This variety needs to be grown
in well-manured, heavy land otherwise it does not make much
cane growth. Sister to 'Malling Jewel', it blooms at the same
time and so misses the late frosts. The berries are large, firm
and sweet and it crops well in heavy soil.

'MALLING JEWEL' The best early-mid-season variety for
frost troubled gardens for its blossom opens later than others.
It bears heavy crops of large, conical fruits of deep red and is
excellent for freezing and bottling.

'MALLING NOTABLE' This follows closely after 'Malling
Jewel' and 'Malling Enterprise', its fruits being large and juicy
but ripening together so that it has only a short season, but
it bridges the gap between the earlies and the lates.

'PYNE'S ROYAL' Introduced in 1907, this has stood the
test of time. It blooms late and misses the frosts whilst its
large, juicy berries are excellent for freezing. It is also the
exhibitor's favourite, but it needs a rich soil to produce
plenty of new canes.

Late

'AMBER QUEEN' Raised in Wiltshire, this makes an abundance of new canes and crops heavily over an extended season,
the large, juicy fruits being orange-yellow, tinted with red.

'GOLDEN EVEREST' A late yellow variety of delicious flavour and bearing heavy crops over a long season.

'MALLING ADMIRAL' Raised by Dr Elizabeth Keep at East Malling, it has 'Malling Promise' for one parent and possesses the same vigour, whilst it is resistant to virus and botrytis. A heavy cropper, it is one of the latest to ripen, extending the season until the autumn fruiting varieties are ready.

'MALLING LANDMARK' The last of the summer varieties, following 'Norfolk Giant' though it does not crop so heavily. Whilst its fruit is difficult to 'plug', its value lies in its lateness.

'NORFOLK GIANT' This blooms late and does well in the most frost troubled gardens, and it is immune to all diseases. Cropping heavily in all soils, it is the best of all for bottling, canning and deep freezing, the fruit being firm but not as sweet as others.

Autumn-Fruiting

'FALLGOLD' A new American variety of vigorous habit and bearing until November, large yellow berries of outstanding flavour.

'NOVEMBER ABUNDANCE' The latest of all but continuing to crop until the frosts; it needs a warm, sunny garden and a well nourished soil. One of the few varieties to receive an Award of Merit, its large red berries possess outstanding flavour.

'SEPTEMBER' An American variety which bears a heavy crop from late August until the end of October, though it ripens its fruit only south of a line from Chester to the Trent. It is tolerant of dry soils and a dry summer when other varieties find difficulty in producing large juicy berries.

'ZEVA' A new Swiss introduction, this is a hardy variety and makes plenty of new canes on which it begins to fruit early in August, continuing until late October. The fruits are large, almost like red blackberries and ripen to deep scarlet. They are sweet and juicy.

4 Gooseberries

This is a fruit that is at its best in a cold climate where the slow ripening brings out the subtle flavour of the fruit. It does better than any fruit in the north, where it has been grown in almost every garden since the friendly rivalry of the gooseberry shows began about the year of Waterloo and made it the most popular of all fruits. It is rarely troubled by frost and is never spoilt by rain, moisture falling off the glossy skins like water off a duck's back. The fruits will hang on the bushes for several weeks and so may be used when slightly under ripe for culinary purposes and when fully ripe for dessert, when it makes as delicious eating as the best strawberries. What is more, the fruits may be picked when the weather or one's time permits and with little fear of them being over-ripe. They also bottle and freeze well. Yet so few of the hundred or so varieties in cultivation are known to modern gardeners and we miss much. Most people only know 'Careless', so much used by the canners while others, such as the olive-skinned 'Broom Girl' which bears fruit almost of golf ball size and is sweet and juicy, are completely ignored.

For an exposed garden, high above sea level, the gooseberry crops well whilst it is suitable to grow in frost hollows too. It is virtually fool-proof and rarely fails to bear heavy crops whatever the weather. By planting for succession it is possible to enjoy the fruit over several months, 'May Duke' and 'Whitesmith' being ready for culinary use at the end of May whilst 'Leveller' and 'Howard's Lancer' will hang until the end of July and often well into August, 'Leveller' being much in demand at this time of year.

SOIL REQUIREMENTS

Soil is important for a good crop, gooseberries preferring a light, well drained soil but one which is well supplied with humus although an excess of nitrogenous manure is to be avoided for it encourages mildew. Work in some peat and garden compost or small quantities of farmyard manure. Humus is necessary to conserve moisture in summer whilst the fruit is swelling and is particularly necessary for dessert varieties which will grow to a considerable size before they are at their best, when they will be sweet and juicy. Culinary varieties do not grow so large nor are they required to do so. The more nitrogen there is in the soil, the cooler will be the roots. For this reason it is most important to add large amounts of humus where growing in a shallow soil, especially over a chalk subsoil.

The plants require only sufficient nitrogen to promote the growth of new wood which may eventually take the place of older wood when the plants have grown big. Those of spreading habit will cover at least a square yard of ground; those of more upright growth will cover about half that area. Gooseberries crop both on the old and new wood, hence a three-year-old plant will bear several pounds of fruit and the quantity will increase each year.

Gooseberries are also potash lovers and as much as 2 oz per plant of sulphate of potash should be given each year in April, as a top dressing. This will enable the plants to grow 'hard' so that they will not be troubled with mildew. It will also improve the quality and flavour of the fruit. Where growing in a heavy loam, only half the amount of potash is required as for light land. It may be given in the form of wood ash stored dry. The potash content is quickly washed down to the roots by rain.

Because gooseberries resent root disturbance and send out their fibrous roots to some distance from the plant, it is essential to plant in clean ground. Where weeds compete with the gooseberries, the quality of the fruit is always poor. Nor is it advisable to hoe too near the plants for fear of damaging the roots. A distance of 15 in $\simeq$ 36 cm from the main stem or leg must be allowed and here, a mulch of peat or garden compost will suppress weeds.

During dry weather, water copiously and to increase the size and quality of dessert varieties, water with liquid manure every ten days, preferably during showery weather. If the soil around the plants is allowed to dry out when the fruits are swelling and water is then given, it will result in split berries. So keep the hose going on the plants to prevent the roots from drying out. Gooseberries respond to artificial watering and feeding more than any other soft fruit.

Where top quality dessert fruit is required, cut back all wood to about two-thirds of its growth each winter or to about 3 in $\backsimeq$ 7·5 cm of the new season's wood. This will direct the energies of the plant to bearing large fruits rather than to the formation of an extension to the shoots. If growing as cordons, and this is an economical way of growing gooseberries, fastening them to strong wires as for cordon apples, prune or pinch back the shoots to within 3–4 in $\backsimeq$ 7–10 cm of their base. This is best done during March, or in severe winters in April.

For culinary varieties e.g. 'Careless' and 'Warrington', the only pruning necessary is to cut out dead wood as it forms, which will not be until the plants are 5–6 years old.

PRUNING

Where pruning those varieties of drooping habit such as 'Whinham's Industry', cut back to an upwards bud to counteract this tendency, whilst those of upright habit are cut back to an outwards pointing bud to prevent overcrowding at the centre. Study each variety and prune accordingly.

If growing for show or if it is desired to have dessert gooseberries of some size, it may be necessary to thin the small fruits where there is overcrowding. 'London', 'Lord Derby' and 'Princess Royal' are varieties which respond to thinning by growing to almost golf ball size. Use the thinnings for culinary purposes.

Gooseberries are grown on a 'leg' to prevent the formation of suckers. If raising plants from cuttings, use only new wood (light in colour) and remove the shoots when about 9 in $\backsimeq$ 23 cm long. Remove all but the top three buds so that the plant will have a good 'leg' and treat the severed end with hormone powder to encourage rooting. It is also important

Winter pruning of standard gooseberries.

to insert them in the rooting medium, which may be a mixture of sand and peat, as quickly as possible, whilst the sap is still in the cuttings and they are moist. If allowed to become dry, they will never root.

The method is to dig a V-shaped trench 6 in $\simeq$ 15 cm deep and to fill it with peat and sand into which the cuttings are inserted 3–4 in $\simeq$ 8–10 cm apart and made firm. Early autumn is the most suitable time and, if the weather is dry, water the cuttings in and whenever the compost shows signs of drying out. If a continuous cloche of p.v.c. sheeting is placed over the trench and closed at both ends, the moist, humid atmosphere will ensure more rapid rooting.

A single cordon is obtained by cutting back lateral shoots to a single bud and growing on the extension shoot until the plant is about 4 ft $\simeq$ 1·20 m tall. Cordons are grown against wires which may be fixed along the side of a path where they will take up little room. They are planted at an oblique angle to restrict the flow of sap. New growth formed during summer should be pinched back to within 2 in $\simeq$ 5 cm of the main stem in August.

A double cordon is made by cutting back the main stem to two buds about 8 in $\simeq$ 20 cm above soil level, each of which face in opposite directions. From the buds, shoots are formed which are first tied to the wires at an angle of 45°, then horizontally. When the shoots have grown about 12 in $\simeq$ 30 cm, they are cut back to an upwards bud and grown on in vertical fashion to whatever height desired, at the end of summer pinching back the newly formed growth of each shoot to about 2 in $\simeq$ 5 cm of the main stems as for single cordons. Red currants may be grown in the same way and they are also grown on a 'leg'.

Gooseberries may be planted at any time during winter, though November is the most suitable time since the plants will have become established before the frosts. Planting distances will depend upon variety, those of upright habit being spaced 4 ft $\simeq$ 1·20 m apart; those of spreading habit 5–6 ft $\simeq$ 1·5–2 m apart each way. Some varieties never make large plants, 'Bedford Red' and 'Langley Gage' retaining their compact habit and being ideal for the small garden, whilst 'Lancashire Lad' and 'Crown Bob' make large spreading bushes and crop heavily so that they are favoured by commercial growers.

Since gooseberries tolerate partial shade, they may be planted between young orchard trees or between rows of raspberries, and strawberries may be grown for several years between the gooseberries until the gooseberries grow too large. Requiring a similar balanced diet of nitrogen and potash, these soft fruits are best grown together. The gooseberries will also provide the strawberries with protection against frost and cold winds for they come early into leaf.

Single cordons are planted 2 ft $\backsimeq$ 60 cm apart and double cordons twice that distance.

Cuttings rooted over winter should be lifted with care so as not to damage the roots and may be planted into their fruiting quarters in April. If they have not by then formed roots, allow them to remain in the trenches until September when they may then be moved. They will take two more years to fruit but strawberries may be planted between the rows and to within 12 in $\backsimeq$ 30 cm of the gooseberries so that the ground will be cropped to advantage. The young gooseberries will respond to a mulch each year after moving to their fruiting quarters, and keep them growing during dry weather by regular waterings. Well looked after, gooseberries will bear heavy crops for thirty years or more and require the minimum attention with their pruning.

Gooseberries ripen yellow, green, white or red, the earliest in May, the latest early August.

VARIETIES
Early
'BEDFORD RED' This makes a plant of neat, upright habit and is ideal for small gardens. The fruit is large and round, ripening to deep crimson.

'BROOM GIRL' Handsome and of outstanding flavour, the large round fruits ripen to deep yellow with green shading. It crops well in all soils.

'EARLY SULPHUR' Making a large spreading bush, this bears heavy crops of pale yellow fruits of outstanding flavour.

'KEEPSAKE' Almost as early as 'May Duke', this makes a large, spreading plant and crops heavily, the white, oval fruits

48

being tinted with green and of excellent flavour.

'LANGLEY GAGE' This outstanding variety received an Award of Merit for its flavour. It makes a neat, upright bush and bears heavy crops of small, white, transparent fruits which are sweet and juicy.

'MAY DUKE' Makes a compact bush and is the earliest variety, ready to pick green in May to use in the kitchen; delicious for dessert in June by which time the fruits have turned deep red.

'WHITESMITH' Very early, this is possibly the best all-round gooseberry, bearing large, white, downy fruits along the whole length of the stems: does well in all soils.

Mid-Season

'BEDFORD YELLOW' Raised by Laxton's, this is of neat upright habit and crops heavily in all soils. The large, hairy berries ripen to deep yellow, streaked with red whilst the flavour is outstanding.

'CARELESS' This is grown in larger numbers than any variety for it is reliable in all soils and bears heavily, the white and oval fruits being excellent for bottling, freezing and all culinary purposes.

'COUSEN'S SEEDLING' Popular with the Kent growers, this bears heavy crops of large, deep golden fruits which are of excellent flavour.

'DAN'S MISTAKE' A chance seedling which has stood the test of time. It makes a large spreading bush and bears heavy crops of pale red, oval fruits, mostly on the previous season's wood.

'GREEN OVERALL' Cropping heavily, this makes a huge berry of delicious flavour whilst the fruits are covered with an attractive greyish down.

'GUNNER' A late mid-season, ripening just before the late varieties. One of the best varieties, the olive green berries are large and of excellent flavour.

'LAXTON'S AMBER' Making a neat upright bush, this bears heavy crops of medium-sized, amber coloured fruits which are sweet and juicy.

'LEVELLER' The Cox's Orange of the gooseberry world, for it crops well only in Sussex and Hampshire and parts of

East Anglia where the soil is to its liking. There it bears heavily, the huge, yellow berries having exceptional flavour. Of spreading habit, it is a late mid-season variety.

'SHINER' Making a neat upright bush, the white berries, shaded green are almost square and are sweet and juicy.

'THUMPER' The sweetest of all green gooseberries, the large, smooth-skinned fruits being like tiny balloons: does well in all districts.

Late

'DRILL' This ripens with 'Leveller' and makes a neat compact bush, the deep green fruits being sweet and juicy.

'HOWARD'S LANCER' The latest of all to ripen, many people believe this to be the best variety ever raised. A strong grower in all soils, it bears heavy crops of large, green berries which are excellent for bottling and freezing.

'LANCASHIRE LAD' This makes a big, spreading bush and bears a large, red berry when ripe, ideal for dessert; for culinary purposes picked early in June it is still green.

'RIFLEMAN' One of the last to mature, the bush is neat and upright but it bears its fruit at the centre, making picking difficult, yet the large, hairy, crimson fruits possess excellent flavour.

'THATCHER' Makes a large, spreading bush of drooping habit, and bears a huge, oblong berry of rich green, dotted all over with red: of exceptional flavour.

'WHINHAM'S INDUSTRY' Making a big spreading plant, this ripens its crimson fruits at the same time as 'Leveller' and they may be used for dessert or culinary purposes.

'WHITE LION' The best white to mature late when it is the equal of 'Leveller' in size and flavour, whilst it bears a heavy crop in all soils.

'WHITE TRANSPARENT' One of the best of the later mid-season varieties, this makes a large but upright bush and bears large crops of huge, white fruits which have a smooth transparent skin and are sweet and juicy.

5 Black and Red Currants

Red and black currants, never as popular as gooseberries, require exactly the opposite conditions and are more exacting in their needs. Whereas gooseberries are at their best in the cold, moist climate of the midlands and north, being frost hardy and tolerant of cold winds, black currants prefer the warmth of the south and of East Anglia where most are grown commercially. Until the introduction of 'Laxton's Giant' which bears fruit of the size of cherries and equally delicious, the popularity of the black currant rested on its culinary value, for making pies and tarts and for preserves. 'Laxton's Giant' has created a new interest in this fruit whilst several varieties which greatly extend the cropping season have removed much of the uncertainty from this crop. Even so, with the plants dropping their fruit buds in cold windy weather, black currants should not be widely planted in the north. If they are to be grown, plant those which mature late and are more tolerant of frost and cold winds, the most reliable being the new 'Cotswold Cross' and 'Wellington XXX'. The varieties 'Baldwin', 'Westwick Choice' and 'Boskoop Giant' should be grown only in the south for 'bud burst' is early.

Select as sheltered a position as possible for the plants and, if cold winds are troublesome, plant near a 'hedge' of hardy blackberries, where the shoots are trained along wires. Whereas gooseberries are happy in partial shade, black and red currants require an open, sunny situation, more so than any soft fruit. Where conditions suit them, black currants will remain productive for thirty years or more.

SOIL REQUIREMENTS

As plant growth is from suckers or underground shoots, black currants are not grown on a leg, though red currants are. With black currants, the stems or shoots are produced from buds which are below soil level and the fruit is borne along the whole length of the canes which grow about 4 ft $\simeq$ 1·20 m tall. It is important to guard against damaging the underground buds by not hoeing too near the plants. It is also necessary to encourage the formation of as much new wood as possible each year and black currants need a long growing season which is not possible in the north. They also need a soil containing plenty of moisture-holding humus and nitrogenous manures for it is nitrogen which encourages plant growth. Black currants always do better in heavy soils as long as they are well drained. Only 'Baldwin' does well on light land and perhaps 'Mendip Cross' which is of 'Baldwin' parentage; also 'Blacksmith'. Other varieties are not so fussy as to soil.

The plants are deep rooting in their search for food and moisture so incorporate as much humus as possible to a depth of at least 20 in $\simeq$ 50 cm. Shoddy, old mushroom-bed compost, farmyard manure and garden compost is suitable for they have a valuable nitrogen content. In addition, work in some peat which will help to encourage a vigorous root run in a heavy soil. Hop manure or used hops from a brewery are useful for opening up a heavy soil whilst they add 'body' to light land, soaking up and retaining moisture in summer. Straw composted with an activator and containing poultry manure, or manure from a pigeon loft will also grow good crops. Heavy land will also be opened up by incorporating some grit or old mortar and clearings from ditches which should be added to the lower 'spit' when the soil is turned over. Those near the coast will find that chopped seaweed augmented by fish meal or fish waste will supply valuable plant foods and if these are in short supply, give each plant a handful of bone meal scattered over the roots at planting time. Poultry keepers should work in feathers which are a valuable source of nitrogen; so, too, is hoof and horn meal. These are all organic manures, rich in nitrogen and they are so much better than inorganic fertilizers for black currants

A healthy crop of black currants like these can only be obtained by careful pruning and cultivation.

never do well in a soil lacking in humus however rich it is in nitrogen. Humus is vital to conserve moisture in summer without which the plants cannot make new wood whilst the fruit will be small and seedy. Because of this, they need a mulch of peat and strawy manure or garden compost placed around each plant in May. This will also suppress weeds around the plant for cultivations should not be nearer than 18 in ≃ 46 cm. The surface roots will reach out to at least this distance.

Where humus is present in quantity, the plants will benefit from a 1 oz per sq. yd dressing of nitro-chalk given in April during showery weather and again in early autumn after old wood is cut out and burnt. It has been found that a second dressing of nitro-chalk given at this time (provided there is plenty of humus in the soil) will greatly increase the yield the following year.

Unlike gooseberries, potash is not required in quantity but if any bonfire ash is applied to the top soil at planting time, this should provide all the potash necessary.

Planting may be done at any time between November and March but if the land is not well drained, March planting is preferable. Distance apart will depend upon variety. For a small garden, for succession, plant 'Mendip Cross', 'Seabrook's' (or 'Westwick Triumph') and 'Amos Black', the latter being the latest of all, ripening its fruit early September. Each of these is of compact habit and may be planted 4–5 ft ≃ 1·20–1·50 m apart without overcrowding. Those of vigorous habit like 'Westwick Choice' and 'Wellington XXX' should be allowed an extra 18 in ≃ 46 cm, both in and between the rows. More economic use of the ground can be made by planting slightly closer in the rows and with greater spacing between the rows so that a double row of strawberries can be planted between. By planting closer in the rows, damage by frost and cold winds is less likely. Be sure that the ground is clear of weeds before planting for to cultivate too near the plants afterwards will be to greatly reduce the crop if the underground buds are damaged.

Black currants are planted about 6 in ≃ 15 cm deep, which is deeper than most soft fruits, and trodden in firmly. Plant when the soil is friable and contains no frost.

CARE AFTER PLANTING

Early March, cut back all wood to about 3 in $\simeq$ 7–8 cm of soil level. This will stimulate the underground buds into growth and a bushy plant will be quickly built up. At the same time tread in any plants lifted from the ground by frost.

It should be said that only reliable plants from a specialist grower should be obtained, guaranteed free from big bud or reversion, a disease caused by the gall mite when the flower buds fail to open and little fruit is obtained. Reliable growers supply 'guaranteed' stock at no extra cost. A two-year-old bush is the best to plant.

Pruning of established plants (and they will bear no fruit the first year) will not be necessary until they have been growing for at least three years. Afterwards, cut out any dead wood or, where there is overcrowding, almost to the base. Also, any unduly long shoots may be cut back to a 'break' bud and the newly formed shoot grown on. This will prevent the older plants from forming too much old wood and so keep them vigorous and healthy.

Black currants are the easiest of soft fruits to propagate, hence they are inexpensive to buy. Later in September, after fruiting has ended, cut out a shoot or two of the new season's wood from each plant and insert just as they are, in trenches of peat and sand as for gooseberries, but remove none of the buds so that all are allowed to form shoots. The cuttings will have rooted by the following April when they can be lifted carefully and planted in their fruiting quarters. Allow them to grow on during summer and in autumn cut back shoots to 3 in $\simeq$ 7–8 cm of the base to build up a bushy plant for the following year. The following year they will come into fruit and if regularly mulched will bear increasing crops for the next thirty years. Regular spraying with Bordeaux mixture will keep the plants free from rust and leaf spot (see Chapter 9).

VARIETIES
Early

'BOSKOOP GIANT'   Raised in Holland, this makes a large, spreading plant, the fruit trusses being long, the berries sweet and juicy but it suffers more than most from frost.

'LAXTON'S GIANT' Its introduction heralded a new break in this fruit for it was the first dessert variety, its sweet and juicy fruit being of the size of a black 'Early Rivers' cherry and to be enjoyed like one. It also bottles well and is delicious in a tart or flan. For the exhibitor it has no equal since it is not only frost and disease resistant but also the first to ripen, in some districts before the end of June. It requires a rich soil to give of its best.

'MENDIP CROSS' Raised from 'Boskoop Giant', this possesses all its good qualities and none of its defects. Making a compact bush, it is resistant to frost and cold winds whilst it bears heavy crops of sweet, juicy fruit.

'WELLINGTON XXX' Where there is room to grow this vigorous variety, it is one of the best, doing well everywhere, especially in East Anglia. Bud burst is late and so it is the best early to mid-season variety for a frost-prone garden whilst it bears heavy crops of thick-skinned fruits which freeze and bottle well.

Mid-Season

'BLACKSMITH' Bud burst is late so this variety may be planted to follow 'Wellington XXX' in frosty areas. It is a reliable and heavy cropper even in light soils, the fruit being borne in long double trusses.

'SEABROOK'S BLACK' Of compact upright habit and though bud burst is early, resistant to frost; also to 'big bud'. It bears its large fruits in trusses of two and three so that it yields heavy crops.

'TENAH' A new Dutch variety which is tolerant of frost and cold winds and bears heavy crops of medium sized fruits.

'WESTWICK TRIUMPH' Of compact habit, bud burst is so late that it may be grown with every chance of heavy crops in those gardens troubled by late frosts. The fruit is large and sweet and borne in very long trusses.

Late

'AMOS BLACK' Making a plant of slender upright habit, this is the best late for a small garden, being the last to ripen its fruit and flowering late it misses all frosts. It bears a heavy crop of medium sized, thick-skinned fruits.

'BALDWIN' If the Hilltop strain is obtained, this is still one of the best lates for a warm garden protected from cold winds. The fruits are extremely juicy and its ability to hold its fruit several weeks after ripening, makes it a valuable garden variety.

'COTSWOLD CROSS' Of the same parentage as 'Amos Black', this is equally good, cropping well in all districts and in all soils and bearing its large, juicy berries in short compact clusters.

RED CURRANTS

At one time grown for their ability to set jam it has, since the extraction of pectin from apples, become less common and is now seen in few gardens, yet for conserves to accompany meats and for pies, few fruits can match it. Growing on a 'leg', like gooseberries, it is not so heavy cropping, whilst the scarlet fruits attract birds so that plants should be covered with muslin when the fruit begins to ripen. Against this, the plants will crop for at least thirty years and are less troubled by pest and disease than any other fruit.

Red currants enjoy the same soil conditions as the goose-berry and are usually grown with them, planting one here and there in the rows. A light, deeply dug soil containing plenty of humus rather than nitrogenous manures suits it best and though it prefers light land, humus is necessary to retain summer moisture without which the fruits remain small and seedy. But with ample moisture they swell as large as black currants and are sweet and juicy.

At planting time, rake in 1 oz of sulphate of potash to each plant or plenty of wood ash which has been stored under cover and this is repeated in April each year. The plants also appreciate a summer mulch given in early June when decayed manure or garden compost, together with some peat is placed around each plant.

Planting is done November–December before hard frosts, setting the plants about 4 ft ≃ 1·20 m apart. Before planting, remove any roots which may have formed up the stem or 'leg' and which might cause suckers to form if left on.

Red currants 'Laxton's No. 1'.

Select a position sheltered from cold winds. They are best planted among gooseberries for protection. For this reason, red currants usually crop better in the south. Plant firmly.

The minimum of pruning is necessary, for like gooseberries, the fruit is borne both on the old and new wood. New shoots are cut back to within 3 in $\approx$ 7–8 cm of the base to encourage fruit buds and to ensure good sized berries. This is done early in spring so that the energy of the plant will be directed to the formation of good fruit whilst at the same time, a compact head will be built up. In later years, any dead wood must be cut out.

Red currants may also be grown (like gooseberries) as single or double cordons in the manner described for goose-berries. In this way, they may be grown against a sunny wall or alongside a path provided they are sheltered from cold winds. Also, they must be in the open, in full sun. They never do well in semi-shade. Single cordons are planted 20 in $\approx$ 50 cm apart, at an oblique angle and tied in to wires; double cordons 3 ft $\approx$ 1 m apart, and here the shoots on either side the 'leg' are grown upright. Small pieces of tin fastened to the wires so that they jingle in the breeze will help to scare off the birds.

To propagate, remove 12 in $\approx$ 30 cm long shoots of the new season's wood about October 1st and after removing all except the upper three buds, treat the base with hormone powder to encourage rooting and plant in a V-trench containing peat and sand. The shoots will take eighteen months to root, after which they are moved to their fruiting quarters in April. They will come into fruit the following year.

VARIETIES
Early
'FAY'S PROLIFIC'   Raised in New York a century ago, this makes a neat, compact bush and is one of the best for northern gardens as it blooms late.

'JONKHEER VAN TETS'   A new Dutch variety making a large plant and cropping heavily, its large, crimson fruits being sweet and juicy.

'LAXTON'S NO. 1'   A strong grower and reliable cropper in all districts, this is the first to mature, the fruits being of rich red though not so large as those of 'Red Lake' which follows it. It does well in all soils.

Mid-Season

'HOUGHTON CASTLE' Raised near Hexham as long ago as 1820, this blooms late and is still widely planted in the north for it misses late frosts. It makes a large, spreading bush and bears heavy crops of sweet crimson berries.

'RED LAKE' Raised in Minnesota, U.S.A., it is, with 'Laxton's No. 1', the most reliable variety for all soils and all districts whilst the berries are of dessert size, being almost as large as black currant, 'Laxton's Giant' and sweet and juicy. The fruit is borne in long trusses.

Late

'WILSON'S LONG BUNCH' The last to ripen and the best late variety forming a bush of spreading habit. It blooms so late as to miss the frosts. The cerise-pink berries are borne in long trusses and are of good size when the plants are well supplied with humus.

WHITE CURRANTS

These require exactly the same culture as red currants and the best variety, flowering late, is 'White Transparent' which bears heavy crops of cream coloured fruits which are sweet and juicy.

6 Blackberries and Hybrid Berries

These are the last of the soft fruits in the season, ripening throughout autumn and extending the season until November. They are also the hardiest, being in no way troubled by frost and cold winds. Indeed, they are usually planted as a wind break, along the side of the garden where the prevailing wind is most felt and here they act as protection for other soft fruits. Blackberries and many hybrid berries which are of blackberry or loganberry parentage freeze well so that there is no waste with the crop, whilst the introduction of thornless varieties is giving them a new popularity.

They may be planted against a sunless wall where few other fruits will grow well, tying in the long arching shoots or branches to trellis or wires. They may be used to cover trellis or rustic fencing which may have been erected to divide one part of the garden from another or to hide a corner where dustbins are kept, whilst 'Himalaya Giant', with its large thorns, may be used for an outer hedge, training the shoots along wires fastened to strong posts driven well into the ground at intervals of 10 ft $\approx$ 3 m. In two years, the plants will have formed a hedge which when 5 ft $\approx$ 1·50 m high will be impenetrable, whilst the weight of fruit will be enormous. They may be planted in this way along the side of the garden against prevailing winds where they will crop heavily. Loganberries, with their brittle wood are not suitable for this purpose and crop better in the more sheltered gardens of the south and west.

The hybrid berries are also planted in rows, allowing 5 ft $\approx$ 1·50 m between each row and planting 10 ft $\approx$ 3 m apart for the more vigorous varieties and 8 ft ≃ 2·40 m for those of less vigour. Where possible, plant thornless varieties for the work of tying in the shoots is less tedious and damaging to the hands.

Another way to grow them is against poles which stand about 6–7 ft ≃ 2 m above ground, with about 3 ft ≃ 1 m buried in the ground. In this way blackberries may be planted between rows of gooseberries and loganberries with black currants for the shoots are grown perpendicular and tied to the poles like climbing roses. About every third year, the shoots are untied and allowed to fall to the ground when any dead wood is cut out before the shoots are tied in again. If logan-berries are grown in this way, the old wood is removed each year in November for they fruit only on the new season's wood. Blackberries and those hybrid berries of blackberry parentage crop both on the old and new wood, hence bear prolifically but the plants will be kept healthier and will bear heavier crops if kept free of too much old wood.

SOIL REQUIREMENTS
Loganberries therefore (and those berries of loganberry parentage) require large amounts of nitrogenous manures to help them produce an abundance of new cane growth each year. This is given as shoddy, farmyard manure, poultry man-ure or garden compost. Feathers, too, are a valuable source of nitrogen. Humus is necessary to maintain moisture in the soil during summer when the plants are making new growth and any manures that can be obtained should be augmented by a quantity of peat. Blackberries do not need to make so much new wood, sufficient only to maintain a balance between the old and the new, so that the plants remain healthy and vigorous. Work in whatever organic manures are available, augmented by some peat and each year give all plants a heavy mulch of garden compost early in May and again in December, when old and dead wood is cut out after fruiting.

Before mulching, give each plant 1 oz of sulphate of potash which is raked into the surface. This is given in April during showery weather. It will improve the quality of fruit and build up a hard plant, better able to withstand cold winds.

Mulching is important and in a dry summer will enable the

plants to produce an extra pound or two of fruit each and at the same time, plenty of new wood. Blackberries form many of their roots just below the surface of the soil and, if shaded from the sun by the mulch which will also keep them moist, the plants will respond by remaining healthy and vigorous for thirty years or more. Lawn mowings are better used for mulching when partly composted. If not, and they are applied thickly, they may heat up and damage the surface roots. The use of a mulch will almost do away with the need to water the plants artificially, though they will appreciate an occasional spraying in hot dry weather, whilst watering with dilute liquid manure every fortnight will increase the weight and quality of the fruit.

Take care not to take the hoe too near the plants for they send out their surface roots to at least 2 ft $\simeq$ 60 cm. Rely on mulching close to the plants to suppress weeds.

The time to prepare the ground and to plant is November–December, usually before hard frost and the plants will be settled in before they begin to make new growth early in spring. Planting, however, may take place whenever the ground is free of frost, until mid-March.

PRUNING

Like raspberries, blackberries and the hybrid berries resent deep planting. Plant only just beneath the surface so that the roots are just covered but make firm by treading in. The posts to which the wires will be fastened at intervals of 18 in $\simeq$ 46 cm from the bottom, or the poles against which the plants will grow, should have been creosoted where they will be below soil level and should be in position before planting so that the roots are not disturbed.

After planting, cut back the stems to within 6 in $\simeq$ 15 cm of soil level to stimulate the plants to form new wood during their first year, tying in the shoots as they form. Blackberries are tied to the wires horizontally, but loganberries which are of more raspberry habit and produce their arching stems (canes) almost upright, are tied to the wires fan-like rather than horizontally for if any attempt is made to bend them unduly, they will snap.

Loganberries also require the same pruning as raspberries,

cutting out the old shoots in November, after fruiting, to 3 in ≃ 7 cm of the base. The new shoots are tied in as they form during summer. The loganberry fruits at the same time as the raspberry, being the first of the hybrid berries to do so. It will crop until the end of August when the first black-berries are ripe.

To propagate blackberries and the hybrid berries of black-berry parentage, simply bend over one or two young shoots from each plant and early in August, bury the tips in the soil to which a little peat is incorporated. Tread firmly and keep the soil moist. By late November, roots will have formed at the tips when they are severed from the parent but left in position until March when they are lifted and replanted where they are to fruit. Loganberries are propagated by lifting a root or two and pulling away the canes as for raspberries.

VARIETIES OF BLACKBERRY
Early
'BEDFORD GIANT' The first of the blackberries to ripen early in August and excellent for freezing. It crops well under all conditions, the large firm fruits being sweet and juicy.

'MERTON EARLY' This variety comes true from seed sown in a cold frame or in drills outdoors in March, the seedlings being moved to nursery beds in August and planted 6 in ≃ 15 cm apart. The plants will be ready to move to their fruiting quarters the following April. The fruit is large and of good flavour whilst the plant is of compact habit and may be planted 6 ft ≃ 1·80 m apart, the canes being grown fanwise like loganberries which it more nearly resembles in that the canes die after fruiting. The fruit is also borne on the new wood.

Mid-Season
'ASHTON CROSS' This ripens its fruit after 'Bedford Giant' and before 'Himalaya Giant' and is a vigorous grower, highly resistant to virus. In good soil it crops heavily, the large round berries being of good flavour.

'HIMALAYA GIANT' This variety possesses extreme hardi-ness and crops heavily both on the old and new wood. Since its introduction in 1900, it has been widely planted as a hedge or wind break but its large thorns make picking difficult. The fruit is large and firm so that it bottles and freezes well.

'OREGON THORNLESS' Likely to supersede all others for mid-season for its fern-like foliage is most handsome, whilst an established plant will yield 10–12 lbs of large juicy berries between mid-September and mid-October. What is more, it is thornless, making picking and tying a pleasure. Is now grown instead of the lighter cropping 'Merton Thornless'.

Late

'JOHN INNES' A late fruiting blackberry, too late for northern gardens except in a warm autumn, for it does not ripen until early October. In the south it crops heavily, whilst cane growth is vigorous and it bears well on the old and new wood.

HYBRID BERRIES

BOYSENBERRY Of American origin and said to be a cross between a loganberry and blackberry with the habit and flavour of the former. A plant of vigorous habit, the large mulberry-red fruits ripen through September.

JAPANESE WINEBERRY A handsome plant, introduced from the East a century ago and perfectly hardy. The soft green leaves are white on the underside whilst the canes are covered with crimson hairs rather than thorns. Could be grown as an ornamental climber. In August it bears masses of golden fruits of raspberry size and of unusual, grape-like flavour.

LAXTONBERRY The result of a cross between the loganberry and raspberry with a similar habit, the canes growing upright and being brittle. In the warmer parts of the U.K., it bears a heavy crop of bright red fruits during late August and September and fruits on the new wood.

LOGANBERRY Believed to be a red variety of the Californian blackberry, *Rubus vitifolius*, this bears a long tapering crimson fruit which does not part from its 'plug' and so retains its shape after bottling and freezing. It must be fully ripe before using. It fruits only on the new wood and since the canes are often troubled by frost and cold winds, it should only be grown south of the Trent. It ripens its fruit during late July and August. The new thornless variety is better in every way, being of more vigorous habit and a pleasure to pick.

LOWBERRY Like Boysenberry, a blackberry–loganberry cross of American origin which fruits on the new wood. The fruits often measure 2 in $\backsimeq$ 5 cm long and are jet black with the aroma of blackberries, whilst it crops heavily in a mild climate.

YOUNGBERRY Another loganberry–blackberry cross and like all those hybrids of this parentage, crops and grows better in a warm garden. The berries ripen purple-black with the loganberry flavour whilst as many as 10 lbs of fruit may be picked from a single plant. It crops from mid-August until late September. There is now a thornless variety which makes for easier cropping.

7 Apples and Pears

Apples and pears are the most widely grown of the top fruits, apples being hardier and better able to set good crops in the north and in gardens exposed to cold winds than pears, which prefer the warmth of the south and west. The apple is native of Europe including Britain, the pear of Southern Europe: in France and Italy it grows to perfection, but here it should be given a warm wall and the warmest part of the garden. Apples can be planted in less favourable places. Flowering later, they are more frost tolerant.

APPLES

Apples grow best in a loamy soil that is well drained. Most difficult are those soils of a limestone nature where there is little depth of top soil. The result is that in a dry year, there is not sufficient moisture for the fruit to grow large and juicy. Such a soil may be made more fertile by green manuring and by adding quantities of decayed manure or garden compost, digging it in as deeply as possible.

APPLES FOR DIFFICULT SOILS
For a limestone soil, 'Barnack Beauty' is the best dessert apple for it crops heavily in such a soil and the fruit will keep until Easter. It makes a large tree and is a tip bearer i.e. it bears its fruits at the end of the shoots rather than on spurs, like 'Cox's Orange Pippin'. Similar in habit is 'Gascoyne's Scarlet' which also does well on chalk. The cream coloured fruit, striped

with scarlet is good both for cooking and dessert if used before Christmas. 'Charles Ross' also does well on chalk and 'Barnack Orange' which is for Christmas dessert.

A heavy, clay soil may be brought into better shape by incorporating clearings from ditches, and any form of organic manure such as shoddy, farmyard manure or old mushroom-bed compost.

For clay soil, 'Adam's Pearmain' is hardy and tolerant of such a soil. Its fruit is mature after Christmas. 'Pott's Seedling', a culinary apple, also does well in clay together with 'Newton Wonder', raised in Derbyshire, and one of the handsomest of all apples. 'Edward VII' is also suitable and will keep until Easter, and, for dessert, 'Herring's Pippin', with its spicy flavour, and 'James Grieve', raised in Scotland.

For wet, low-lying land, work in as much drainage material as possible and some peat and decayed manure. For such a soil, the finest dessert apple is 'Laxton's Superb', at its best in December and for culinary use, 'Grenadier', the best of all pollinators for 'Bramley's Seedling'. 'Lord Derby' also does well in wet soils.

To bring a light, sandy soil into condition, dig in plenty of humus in any form as this will hold the moisture about the roots in summer. Such a soil will usually be deficient in potash so rake in some wood ash or give 1 oz of sulphate of potash spread around each tree after planting. In light soils, for dessert, plant 'Ellison's Orange' which makes a compact tree and comes quickly into bearing; and 'Cox's Orange' and its pollinator 'Worcester Pearmain', the latter making a large tree and being tip bearing. The new 'Acme' is also suitable as is the heavy-cropping 'Pearl'. For kitchen use, plant 'Forge', its greasy-skinned fruit keeping into the New Year.

Planting may be done whenever the ground is in a friable condition between November and March, the earlier the better so that the trees will become established before the frosts. There should be about 6 in $\approx$ 15 cm of soil over the lower roots. Too shallow planting will cause the roots to dry out in a hot summer; too deep planting will mean that the roots are in the less fertile subsoil. It is important to make the hole large enough to allow the roots to be spread well out after shortening the tap root or any unduly long roots. Over them, place a

RIGHT Fan trained apple tree
BELOW Fan trained apple tree in
full fruit

ABOVE Pear 'Conference'
BELOW Pear 'Gorham' espalier trained

spadeful of sand and peat and replace the soil, treading firmly.

Rootstocks play a part in planting distances. 'Malling IX' and 'MM 104' produce a dwarf tree which comes quickly into bearing. Both are used for cordon and pyramid trees. Plant cordons 3 ft $\simeq$ 1 m apart; pyramids 6 ft $\simeq$ 1·80 m. 'MM 109' is now used for bush and standard trees (these with a 5–6 ft $\simeq$ 1·50–1·80 m stem); also 'MXXVI'. Trees on these root-stocks grow large but take longer to bear heavily. In bush form, plant 12 ft $\simeq$ 4 m apart; 20 ft $\simeq$ 6 m as standards.

TYPES OF TREE
Spur forming apples may be planted as cordons alongside a path where they take up little room. They are trained against wires and are planted at an oblique angle to limit growth. Do not plant tip bearers as cordons. Maiden or one-year-old trees are planted, allowing the leader shoot to grow on to 6–7 ft $\simeq$ 1·80 m. In August, pinch back lateral shoots to 6 in $\simeq$ 15 cm of the main stem to build up fruiting spurs as quickly as possible. They will begin to fruit in their second year after planting.

Bush trees are pruned to the open centre plan. Here, the main lateral is cut back to 20 in $\simeq$ 50 cm when laterals are formed below this point which will grow on to become the branches. Allow them to grow on for two years, then 'tip' them so that each stem will then form laterals and these are cut back to half way each year.

The dwarf pyramid form is now popular. With this, a com-pact, heavy cropping tree is built up in the quickest time. To make the buds 'break' on the main stem, a cut is made in the bark just above each and the leader is cut out when the tree is about 3 ft $\simeq$ 1 m tall. At the end of summer, all side shoots are cut back to half the new season's wood, whilst any new fruiting buds formed on the leader are rubbed out.

A standard is bought as a two-year 'feathered' tree, feathers being the small shoots which grow from the stem. This is allowed to grow to about 6 ft $\simeq$ 2 m in height, the feathers being removed. The leader shoot is then removed and the head built up as for bush trees.

Pears are treated in the same way but may also be grown

Heeling in fruit trees.

against a wall or along wires in the espalier or horizontal
form. They take up little space. Here, too, maidens are
planted, the leader being shortened to about 18 in ≃ 46 cm
above ground, to a point where there are two buds, one on
either side of the stem. These will form the first arms or tier
and are allowed to grow to any length until reaching the arms
of the next plant which will be 20 ft ≃ 6 m apart, the arms
eventually reaching to 10 ft ≃ 3 m. As they grow, the arms are
tied to the wires whilst the extension shoot is allowed to grow
on for another 18 in ≃ 46 cm before it is again cut back to
two opposite buds. These will form the second pair of arms
and so the tree is built up to the required height, usually one

tier being formed each year. If growing against the wall of a house, the tree may be grown to a height of 30–40 ft ≃ 8–10 m and each year bear a huge crop.

When the first tier has formed, in its second season, all side growths are pinched back at the end of summer to 5 in ≃ 13 cm of the arms. This will encourage the plant to form fruiting buds instead of more new wood and it will begin to crop the following year. Fruiting will be further encouraged if the arms are also cut back to about half the new wood in December, making the cut to a bud which will grow on to form the new wood and following year.

If, as sometimes happens, a bud will fail to 'break', which would mean the loss of an arm or a badly balanced tree, it will be necessary to persuade the bud to 'break' by making a notch and removing the bark immediately above it.

SOIL REQUIREMENTS
Apples and pears will benefit from a mulch of strawy manure given in spring and spread around the trees. Before it is applied, give each tree a sprinkling of sulphate of potash for this will encourage the formation of fruiting spurs and will improve the quality of fruit. A balanced diet is necessary; nitrogen to make new wood and potash, which when present in the soil, will release the phosphates, essential if the fruit is to grow to a good size. If established trees are not making sufficient growth, in March give each a 1 oz dressing of sulphate of ammonia, raking it into the surface. This will stimulate the trees into growth. The potash can be given with it. 'Newton Wonder', 'Grenadier' and 'Cox's Orange' often show signs of potash deficiency on light land when the foliage turns brown and curls up at the edges.

Apples may also show signs of magnesium deficiency when the leaves turn pale green and fall before their time. If uncorrected, the trees become stunted. If observed, spray the trees in June with a solution of magnesium sulphate (Epsom salts), half a pound dissolved in 2 gallons of water when the magnesium will be absorbed through the leaves. If a handful of fishmeal is lightly forked into the soil around the trees, this contains all the plant foods and can be followed by a summer mulch of decayed manure or composted straw.

Standards will need staking, unless the garden is sheltered. Use 1 in $\simeq$ 25 mm × 1 in $\simeq$ 25 mm timber driven well into the ground and reaching to just beneath the head. It is better to put the stake in place after planting and before covering in the roots. For a tie, use a piece of old tyre inner tubing or one of the special rubber or plastic ties. It is important that the tree does not rub against the stake.

POLLINATION

Before ordering the trees, some thought must be given to pollination. It is no use planting a row of cordon 'Cox's Orange Pippin' and expecting to enjoy heavy crops without a suitable pollinator. With 'Cox's' it has been proved that where 'Worcester Pearmain', 'James Grieve' and 'Egremont Russet' are used for its pollination (one tree to six 'Cox's'), the setting of fruit is twice that obtained by using any other pollinators.

Where certain varieties are required, make sure they will pollinate each other and it is usual that varieties in bloom at the same time will do so. For example, where frosts are troublesome, it is better to plant late flowering varieties such as 'Crawley Beauty' and 'Edward VII', amongst the best of all keepers and with them may be planted 'Lane's Prince Albert' which flowers over a longer season than any other apple. In a good year when there are plenty of pollinating insects about, one or two apples will set their own pollen. These include 'Rev. Wilks' (early), 'Sunset' and 'Grenadier' (mid-season) and 'Crawley Beauty' (late). They are a good selection for all purposes.

Where looking for pollinators, remember that several varieties tend to biennial fruiting, bearing heavily one year, little the next and in the 'off' year there will be little blossom to give of its pollen. 'Newton Wonder', 'D'Arcy Spice', 'Rev. Wilks' and 'Miller's Seedling' are amongst them. Also, several apples are triploids and cannot pollinate others or themselves and so require to be planted with two other varieties (which are not triploids) so as to be able to pollinate each other. The best pollinator for 'Bramley's Seedling', a triploid, is 'Grenadier'; others are 'Ribston Pippin' and 'Gravenstein', which are pollinated by 'Lord Lambourne';

74

and 'Blenheim Orange' which is pollinated by 'Egremont Russet'. These apples flower early and should not be grown in frost-troubled gardens.

Pollination compatibility table:

Key:

T.SS = Triploid: Self sterile	PSF = Diploid: Partly self-fertile
'Beauty of Bath' (PSF)	'Lord Lambourne' (PSF)
'Gladstone' (PSF)	'Miller's Seedling' (PSF)
'Gravenstein' (T.SS)	'Rev. W. Wilks' (PSF)
'Laxton's Fortune' (PSF)	'Ribston Pippin' (T.SS)

These flower early mid-season:

'Annie Elizabeth' (PSF)	'Ellison's Orange' (PSF)
'Arthur Turner' (PSF)	'Grenadier' (PSF)
'Bramley's Seedling' (T.SS)	'James Grieve' (PSF)
'Cox's Orange Pippin' (PSF)	'Tydeman's E. Worcester' (PSF)
'Egremont Russet' (PSF)	'Worcester Pearmain' (PSF)

These flower late mid-season:

'Blenheim Orange' (T.SS)	'Lane's Prince Albert' (PSF)
'Charles Ross' (PSF)	'Laxton's Superb' (PSF)
'Claygate Pearmain' (T.SS)	'Newton Wonder' (PSF)
'Howgate Wonder' (PSF)	'Sunset' (PSF)

These gloom late:

'Court Pendu Plat' (PSF)	'Edward VII' (PSF)
'Crawley Beauty' (PSF)	'Royal Jubilee' (PSF)

Any planted together in each section will ensure satisfactory pollination.

With pears, the same rules apply though they do require greater warmth to crop well and to ripen the fruit properly. Yet there is no reason why the hardier varieties e.g. 'Jargonelle', 'Catillac' and 'Durondeau' cannot be grown in

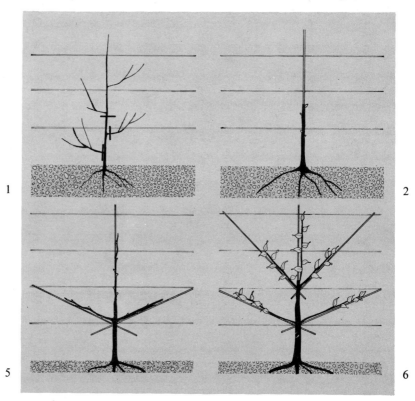

1

2

5

6

A sequence showing the use of canes in the training of a fruit tree.

the cooler parts and also 'Laxton's Superb' and 'William's Bon Cretien' if planted against a warm wall. These pears are hardy and only bloom late but all pears bloom at least two weeks before apples and are more susceptible to frost damage. And whilst there are several apples which bear well in a lime-stone soil, there are no pears which grow well in such a soil. Pears require a soil containing more humus than apples for they must never lack moisture at the roots, especially where growing against a wall, so work in plenty of decayed manure, garden compost or composted straw.

The same rules of pollination apply to pears as to apples. It is advisable to plant near each other several trees which bloom at the same time for there will be few pollinating insects

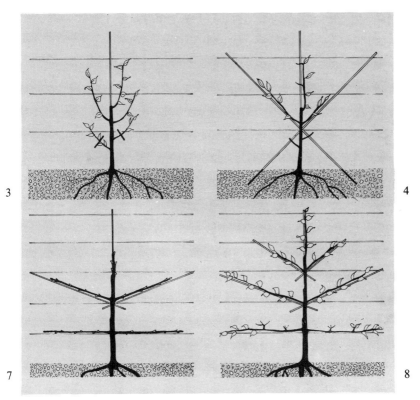

3   4

7   8

about, especially when the first blossom appears. Those hardy pears, 'Jargonelle', 'Catillac' and 'Pitmaston Duchess' are triploids and cannot set their own pollen or that of their pollinator so plant two pollinators with any of these. And remember that the fertile 'Conference' will not pollinate 'Beurre d'Amanlis', and 'Seckle' will not pollinate 'Louise Bonne', though both bloom together.

Pear pollination compatibility table:

Key:
SS = Self sterile   SF = Self-fertile

These pears bloom early and should be omitted from frost-troubled gardens:

'Beurré Easter' (SS)	'Conference' (SF)
'Beurré Hardy' (SS)	'Durondeau' (SF)
'Beurré Superfin' (SF)	'Louise Bonne' (SF)

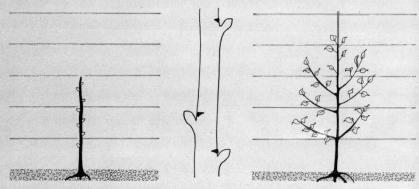

The training of fruit trees. The first illustration shows the plant in April of its 1st year after planting, showing where the shoots should be nicked. The second is a close-up showing where the shoots need to be nicked. The next illustration shows the plant having made growth. The following picture shows the shoot being tied down to the supporting canes in April

Though a number are self-fertile, they will set a greater amount of fruit if grown with others in bloom at the same time. Pears to plant for succession; the best in their season:

Early
'LAXTON'S SUPERB' The best early pear but it must be harvested late August as soon as ripe. If left too long, the fruit will deteriorate. A pear is ripe when placed in the palm of the hand and upon gently lifting, it parts from the tree. In this

78

These pears bloom mid-season:

'Beurré Bedford'	(SF)	'Josephine de Malines'	(SS)
'Clapp's Favourite'	(SS)	'Thompson'	(SS)
'Glou Morceau'	(SS)	'William's Bon Cretien'	(SF)

These pears bloom late:

'Doyenne du Comice'	(SS)	'Laxton's Superb'	(SF)
'Dr Jules Guyot'	(SF)	'Marie Louise'	(SF)
'Fertility'	(SS)	'Winter Nelis'	(SS)

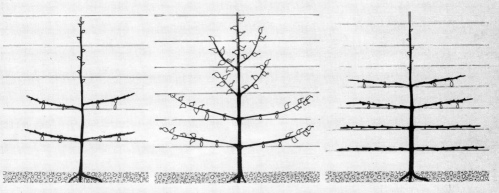

of the 2nd year, and the nicking of the buds on the new leader. The next illustration shows growth made during the 2nd growing season and the last illustration shows a tree being tied down and nicked again in April in the 3rd year after planting.

case, it will be when the green skin takes on a yellow tint. Of neat, upright habit, it blooms late and misses the frosts.

To Ripen September

'DR JULES GUYOT' Flowering late, this is a good pollinator for most late flowering pears whilst it crops best in the dry climate of eastern England. Its large yellow skinned fruits are dotted with black.

'TRIOMPHE DE VIENNE' Hardy and reliable, cropping

well in most years and bearing heavily from a small tree, its highly coloured fruit having good flavour.

'WILLIAM'S BON CRETIEN' It is the Bartlett pear of the American canners and though over 200 years old, it remains one of the best pears ever raised, cropping well everywhere, its musky flavour is renowned. It should be picked green.

To Ripen October

'BRISTOL CROSS' Ready about October 1st, this is a new pear of merit cropping well in the west, its fruit with its white flesh being tender and juicy.

'CONFERENCE' The most reliable of pears, it is a valuable pollinator for mid-season varieties and bears heavy crops, the dark green fruits being russeted when ripe.

To Ripen November

'DURONDEAU' Making a compact tree of great hardiness, the fruit ripens to deep gold with a crimson cheek and will keep until late November.

'LOUISE BONNE' This makes a large tree and crops heavily but only in the warmth of the south-west. The green fruit has red flesh and outstanding flavour.

To Ripen December–January

'PACKHAM'S TRIUMPH' A vigorous grower and free cropper, the fruit is similar in appearance and flavour to 'Comice' but is without that pear's difficulties in culture and should be planted instead.

'SANTA CLAUS' One of the largest pears of excellent flavour, and with an attractive, dull-crimson, russeted skin. It makes a large tree, bears well and is resistant to scab.

To Ripen March–April

'CATILLAC' This pear blooms late, is a vigorous grower and crops well but needs 'Beurré Hardy' and 'Dr Guyot' for its pollination. The large, dull crimson fruits should not be harvested until late November and, if stored in a temperature of 40–45 °F., will keep until Easter.

8 Peaches, Cherries and Plums

Peaches, cherries and plums are the most important of the stone fruits, requiring a soil containing plenty of lime. They are the most reliable fruits for planting in a limestone soil, in which apples (with but one or two exceptions) and pears rarely do well. They all grow a crop well in East Anglia; in Kent and Sussex; and in Hereford and Worcestershire where cherry orchards in bloom are a familiar sight of early summer.

PEACHES

Peaches require a sunny situation, sheltered from cold winds when they may be grown as bush trees in the open. In the less favourable parts, grow in the fan-shape against a sunny wall. They require no manure apart from a little bone meal but plenty of lime rubble must be worked into the soil for peaches will not crop well without it.

Planting is done in November, allowing 18 ft $\simeq$ 6 m for fan trees and 15 ft $\simeq$ 5 m in the bush form. Take out a hole large enough for the roots to be spread well out and, as the soil is replaced, sprinkle in it 2 oz of bone meal for each tree. The variety will have been grafted on to 'Brompton', 'Pershore' or 'Common Mussel' plum rootstocks so when planting, make sure that the union or graft is above soil level so that it will not form roots here. Plant firmly and keep the trees well supplied with moisture during summer. Evaporation of moisture from the soil will be reduced if in May, the plants are given a thick mulch of decayed manure or garden compost, together with some peat. It is essential that the trees do not lack moisture whilst the fruits are swelling.

PRUNING

The peach bears its fruit on the previous year's wood and there will be little fruit if the wood has not been well ripened by the sun. At the end of May, new growth formed by the leader shoots is cut back by about one-third whilst in mid-summer, the tips of the side growths are pinched out when about 3 in $\simeq$ 8 cm long. A single wood bud will be retained at the base of each shoot to grow on as a replacement for next year's fruit, the shoot which has borne fruit being removed at the end of the season though during the first years of the tree, fruiting shoots are allowed to grow on until reaching 18 in $\simeq$ 46 cm. This is fastened to the wall (or to wires) and the tip pinched back to a wood bud and on the shoot formed here will be borne the next year's crop. Where possible, select a wood bud facing the wall for the extension shoots. Wood buds are small and pointed; blossom buds are fat and round.

Peaches must be encouraged to produce as much new wood as possible for if the old wood is not continually cut out, the plants will soon stop bearing. Also peaches 'bleed' badly where the old wood is cut out, thus reducing the vitality of the plant so encourage as much new wood as possible.

Shoots appearing next to a fruit are pinched out above the second leaf and this removal of unwanted growth should be spread over the whole of June.

Thinning of overcrowded fruit must not be done until after 'stoning'. This is a natural falling off of fruits when they are about the size of a walnut, and it may not be necessary to remove others, though there should be about 6 in $\simeq$ 15 cm between each of those fruits left to mature.

The fruit is ripe when the palm of the hand is placed under it and it will part from the stem when gently lifted upwards. Be gentle when handling and place each fruit on a layer of cotton wool in a shallow box. The fruits must not touch each other or they will decay.

After the fruit is harvested, any dead or unwanted wood is removed and the replacement shoots tied in so that they will not be broken by winter winds.

A fan-trained peach tree in full fruit.

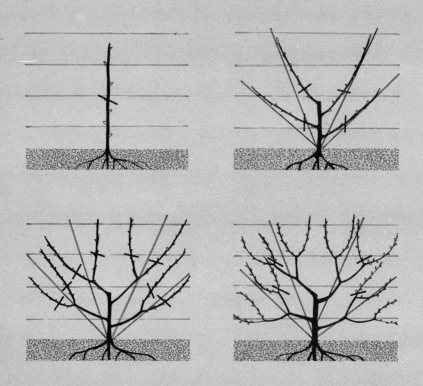

Stages in the shaping of a fan-trained tree, in its 1st, 2nd, 3rd and 4th years.

Peaches do not need pollinators to help them set fruit but on all dry days it is advisable to go over each flower with a camel hair brush. Artificial pollination is a valuable assurance against crop failure, when in a cold year there are few pollinating insects about. Then, if the winds are cold or late frosts persist, hang pieces of muslin over the plants, removing them on warmer days or when the cold spell has gone.

In a warm summer, the first peaches will be ripe by the end of July; the later 'Sea Eagle' not until mid-October, and so it is grown only in the warmer parts and under glass. If in doubt about ripening, plant the early 'Duke of York' or the reliable 'Peregrine' which ripens shortly after.

VARIETIES

'BARRINGTON' An old and strong growing peach, ripening its large pale yellow fruits towards the end of September but in a sunless year tending to be too late outdoors in all but the warmest gardens.

'DUKE OF YORK' The first to ripen, this peach makes the largest fruit. It is deep crimson and of excellent flavour. The most reliable cropper if given a warm wall.

'EARLY RIVERS' One of the earliest, ripe by the end of July, its lemon-yellow skin and white flesh possessing excellent flavour.

'HALE'S EARLY' Early in August its fruit has ripened to deep orange. It bears heavy crops of medium sized fruits of good flavour.

'PEREGRINE' Making a large crimson fruit when ripe, this matures about mid-August and is a reliable cropper.

CHERRIES

Cherries are more exacting in their requirements than any fruit. They crop well only as standards or half standards and as fan-trained trees against a wall, whilst they take almost ten years to bear reasonable crops. They also make large trees as standards, too large for a small garden. Also, none are able to set fruit with their own pollen and only certain varieties will pollinate each other. Again, birds are a constant worry and if the trees do set a good crop, usually half will be taken. Commercial growers employ bird scarers but the amateur can do little about it apart from tying tins together up in the trees when they will scare some birds away. Cherries also bloom early and may be caught by frosts but in a good year they remain in bloom longer than any fruit and at least some will miss the frosts.

SOIL REQUIREMENTS

Cherries do well in a dry sunny climate and do not crop well north of the Trent. A too rich soil causes excessive gumming when the trees are pruned and an excess of foliage with little fruit. In a lime deficient soil, work in plenty of lime rubble or mortar before planting in November, allowing 20 ft $\backsimeq$ 6 m between the trees if standards. Cherries love potash, so work in to the top soil 2 oz of sulphate of potash for each tree and each year in April, give the trees a 1 oz dressing. Wood ash is an alternative but must have been stored dry for the potash content to be still available.

When planting and pruning cherries, which is done in spring, take care not to damage the bark or bacterial canker or silver leaf may enter the wound causing the tree to die back. Cherries need little pruning; merely cut out any old and decayed wood and burn the cuttings.

Before planting, attention must be given to pollinators. Each variety has a flowering period of eighteen days, compared with ten days with plums. Almost a month (28 days) covers the flowering of cherries from the earliest to the latest and all the flowering times overlap, yet play little part in pollinating each other. Here is a list of suitable pollinators for the best garden varieties:

Variety	Pollinators
'Amber Heart'	'Bigarreau Napoleon'; 'Roundel Heart'; 'Waterloo' (and each of these is pollinated by 'Amber Heart' and by each other)

Cherries ripen most successfully in a dry, sunny climate

The healthy bloom on these gages shows that they are ready for picking

'Bradbourne Black'	'Bigarreau Napoleon'; 'Roundel Heart'
'Early Rivers'	'Emperor Francis'; 'Governor Wood'; 'Waterloo'; 'Merton Heart'
'Florence'	'Bigarreau Napoleon'; 'Waterloo'
'Knight's Early Black'	'Amber Heart'; 'Bigarreau Napoleon'; 'Waterloo'
'Merton Heart'	'Early Rivers'; 'Emperor Francis'

Flowering times of the most popular varieties:

V. Early to Bloom:	'Early Rivers'; 'Emperor Francis'; 'Waterloo'
Mid-season blooming:	'Frogmore'; 'Governor Wood'; 'Knight's Early Black'
Late blooming:	'Amber Heart'; 'Bradbourne Black'; 'Roundel Heart'; 'Bigarreau Napoleon'

The most reliable pollinators are:

'Amber Heart'	'Emperor Francis'
'Bigarreau Napoleon'	'Roundel Heart'
'Early Rivers'	'Waterloo'

These will not pollinate each other:

'Early Rivers' and 'Knight's Early Black'
'Elton Heart' and 'Governor Wood'
'Frogmore' and 'Waterloo'

VARIETIES

'AMBER HEART' The best all-round cherry. It is hardy and flowering late it misses the frosts whilst it is a reliable cropper, the large round yellow fruits flushed with red being ripe about mid-July. The 'White Heart' cherry of the London barrow boys.

'BIGARREAU NAPOLEON' A reliable variety, the large bright red fruits ripening early August.

'BRADBOURNE BLACK' Does everything on a large scale, making a big tree, bearing heavily whilst it bears the largest of all cherries which are crimson-black. It blooms late and misses the frosts and is one of the last to ripen, at the end of August.

'EARLY RIVERS' It makes a spreading tree and bears heavily, the large jet black fruits being first to ripen before the end of June. Plant it with 'Merton Heart' which will crop a month later.

'KNIGHT'S EARLY BLACK' Pollinated by most varieties except 'Early Rivers', this makes a compact tree and crops heavily, its jet black fruits being ripe early July.

'MERTON HEART' A new cherry for mid-July and proving a heavy and consistent cropper, its large deep crimson fruits being sweet and juicy. Also pollinated by 'Roundel Heart'.

'ROUNDEL HEART' Plant with 'Waterloo' for they pollinate each other and both make small trees. The large purple fruits are ready mid-July.

'WATERLOO' A good pollinator for so many cherries hence its value but it does not bear so heavily as others. Its deep crimson fruits are ripe mid-July.

Where cherries are grown against a wall, they will reach a height of 10 ft $\simeq$ 3 m or more and to the same distance on either side. After filling the wall, further shoots are removed entirely whilst all side growths are pinched back in mid-June to six-leaves and are again cut back to half-way early in spring. Fruit is borne on both the old and new wood.

Morello cherries, which are excellent for bottling and stewing with sugar for they have a sharp flavour, are valuable in that they may be grown against a north wall in the fan shape. Of great hardiness, they may also be grown as low bushes or used for a hedge but since they fruit only on the new season's wood, much of the old wood is best removed early in spring. They are self-fertile and crop well without a pollinator.

The variety known as 'Kentish Red' bears larger fruit and is just as hardy but needs planting with the Morello for its pollination.

PLUMS AND GAGES

Plums are the most accommodating of the stone fruits, growing well as bush and standard and half standard trees and also in the fan shape against a south or west wall. Here should be planted the gages and best dessert plums. They do well in a warm dry summer following a cold winter, the two extremes suiting plums. Being early flowering, plums should not be planted in a frost hollow. They are happier on higher ground provided they are protected from cold winds. Where frosts are experienced, plant the later-flowering varieties such as 'Oullin's Golden Gage' and 'Belle de Louvin'.

SOIL REQUIREMENTS
Plums do best in a heavy loam and like all stone fruits, do well over a chalky sub-soil. If lime is not present, give a good dressing with lime rubble or mortar before planting for in this form, lime is absorbed by the tree over a long period.

To plant a wall tree, take out a hole 18 in $\simeq$ 46 cm deep and place at the bottom some mortar and over it an upturned turf. Spread out the roots and cover with soil to which has been incorporated either some decayed manure, or a handful of bone meal. The stem should be 6 in $\simeq$ 15 cm from the wall and make sure that the scion is 3 in $\simeq$ 8 cm above the surface when the soil has been filled in and made firm. November is the best time to plant and in April give the plants a 1 oz dressing of sulphate of potash. Above all, give a thick mulch each year in early summer. This will provide the plant with nitrogen and help to conserve moisture in the soil without which wall plants will not do well. Plums make considerable growth and are copious drinkers. They will soon reach a height of 10 ft $\simeq$ 3 m and the same in width and bear fruit all along the wood. The shoots are tied to the wall about 9 in $\simeq$ 23 cm apart.

Very little pruning is needed and if necessary, it is done in March as the tree comes into life after its winter rest, when the cuts heal quickly. The Silver Leaf Disease Order demands that

A fan-trained 'Early Laxton' plum.

all pruning is done by July 15th. This consists of the removal of dead wood and shortening unduly long shoots which must be burnt. Early in summer, side shoots are pinched back to encourage the formation of fruiting spurs.

Some plums are self-fertile and will set fruit with their own pollen; others are only partly so; and some are self-sterile and set fruit only with a pollinator. However, all will set heavier crops where provided with a pollinator. Plums flower only for 18–20 days and apart from those which bloom very early and others very late, most will overlap but as they bloom for a shorter time than any other fruit, they may be seriously harmed by frost.

VARIETIES
Ripe Late July–Early August
'BLACK PRINCE' Hardy and resistant to silver leaf, this makes a small compact tree and bears a large crop of small black fruits, like damsons and with the same flavour.

'CZAR' Resistant to frost for it blooms late yet matures early, cropping well in exposed gardens. The bright purple fruit can be used for cooking at the end of July, for dessert early August.

'DENISTON'S SUPERB' This is used as a pollinator for many plums and gages and is ripe early to mid-August, the round gage-like fruits being deep green, flushed with crimson and with the true gage flavour.

Ripe Mid-End August
'OULLIN'S GOLDEN GAGE' The best gage for this time, its round fruits ripening to golden yellow. It blooms late and is valuable for gardens troubled by frost.

'VICTORIA' The most vigorous and heavy-cropping of all plums. It is self-fertile and pollinates many varieties. Like 'Czar', it crops well in clay soils, its large egg-shaped fruits ripening to pinkish-red.

Ripe in September
'BRYANSTON GAGE' This makes a large tree and crops well in fan-shape, bearing in late September, round greenish fruits speckled with russet.

'COUNT ALTHANN'S GAGE' This bears well in all forms and is pollinated by 'Thames Cross'. The large, round, crimson-purple plums have the true gage flavour.

'LAXTON'S DELICIOUS' A vigorous and hardy variety, bearing heavy crops of large, bright red plums of dessert quality.

'THAMES CROSS' This makes a vigorous tree and is a reliable cropper, its large golden plums being of dessert quality.

DAMSONS

Extremely hardy, damsons crop well in the most exposed gardens and may be planted as a wind break. They also crop well in shallow, stony ground and are rarely troubled by frosts. Plant 8–10 ft $\simeq$ 2·5–3 m apart and do no pruning apart from the occasional removal of dead wood.

The best variety is 'Merryweather' for it sets its own fruit which ripens in early October to blue-black and is of large size. When stewed, it has the true damson flavour. It makes a broad spreading tree.

9 Pests and Diseases

APPLES

Pests

APHIS (GREENFLY)   The green insects attack all fruits and lay their eggs on the plants where they winter, emerging in spring to feed on the young shoots and causing leaf curl. Spray with tar-oil in January or in April with Abol-X or Sybol and again in June.

APPLE SUCKER   This resembles the greenfly and lays and feeds on the fruit spurs in autumn, later on the flower buds causing them to turn brown. The eggs are destroyed by tar-oil in January, or spray with Lindex in April.

BLOSSOM WEEVIL   The grubs eat into the flower buds early in summer so that they fail to open. The black insects winter in the bark. Spraying with tar-oil should give control; or early March, spray with Fentro or Lindex.

CODLING MOTH   This is responsible for the maggoty condition of apples, its presence indicated by a pile of brown dirt at the point of entry when the fruit will be riddled with holes right through. The moth lays its eggs in June and July. To prevent an attack, spray the trees early July with liquid derris or Fentro (based on fenitrothion) which has replaced DDT.

TORTRIX MOTH   The caterpillars attack apples and pears, causing the leaves to curl up at the edges. Defoliation occurs whilst the grubs weave a silken web over the flowers which die. It is one of the most destructive of fruit pests. As routine, spray early May and again in June and July with Abol-X.

WINTER MOTH   Hibernating in the soil, these make their way up the tree stem in mid-winter and if unchecked, feed on the blossom and leaves. About July 1st, they fall to the ground to pupate, the moths emerging in winter. Grease-banding the trees in October will trap many. As an additional precaution, spray with tar-oil in January.

WOOLLY APHIS   Also known as American Blight, this produces a grey, woolly substance under the branches where the pests winter and lay their eggs in spring, causing the branches to swell and crack. Spray with tar-oil in January or with a malathion preparation in the green bud stage.

DISEASES

BROWN ROT   This occurs on the spurs as brown spores causing them to die back whilst the fruit will turn brown in storage. Burn all diseased fruits and spray with lime-sulphur whilst the buds are still green in March. Lime-sulphur should not be used on 'Cox's Orange', 'Newton Wonder' and 'Egremont Russet'.

CANKER   This attacks all top fruits but mostly those growing in badly drained soil, appearing as red bodies which encircle a branch, causing it to die back at this point. 'Bramley's' and 'Grenadier' are highly resistant. To control, remove the entire branch at the point of intersection with the main stem and treat the wound with 'Medo'. Attend to plums and cherries only in spring.

SCAB   This attacks apples and pears given too much nitrogen, appearing on fruit and leaves as pale green spots and is most active in a wet season. It winters on fallen fruits and prunings which should be burnt. To prevent, spray with Orthocide at green-bud stage.

BLACKBERRY AND LOGANBERRY

Pests

APHIS   The insects sometimes collect on the tips of the shoots (canes) or cluster beneath the leaves, sucking the sap and reducing the vitality of the plants. To prevent, spray with tar-oil in January.

RASPBERRY BEETLE   See under Raspberry.

Disease

CANE SPOT The most troublesome disease affecting both old and new wood, causing it to break off and the fruit buds to fall off before opening. To prevent, spray with Bordeaux mixture in April or May before the fruit begins to set.

BLACK CURRANT

Pests

GALL MITE The most troublesome pest which causes big bud. Where present, the mite is there in thousands though visible only through a microscope, the buds being swollen with them. The only known cure is by spraying in early spring with lime-sulphur diluted to 1 part in 50 of water but it should not be used on 'Wellington XXX', 'Westwick Triumph' and 'Blacksmith'.

GREEN CAPSID BUG The eggs winter on older plants and hatch out in April, the bugs feeding on the leaves and buds. It is killed with tar-oil in January.

LEAF MIDGE It is present when the leaf edges roll up and here the midges lay their eggs. Care must be taken (see Gall Mite) if using lime-sulphur on black currants. Preferably spray with liquid derris in May. Never use Lindex or Gamma-BHC on black currants.

Diseases

LEAF SPOT In a wet year, this may attack the stems and foliage as brown spots, causing the leaves to fall prematurely. To control, spray with Bordeaux mixture or Orthocide after picking the fruit.

RUST This appears as orange spots under the leaves causing them to fall and the plant to lose vitality. After picking the fruit, spray with Bordeaux mixture.

CHERRY

Pests

CHERRY SLUGWORM This is the green larva of the cherry sawfly which lays her eggs on the leaves in July (after wintering in the ground), causing them to turn brown. After fruiting, spray with liquid derris every fortnight until mid-September.

FRUIT MOTH   The small green caterpillars enter the buds as they open and later, bore into the fruits making them unusable. The moths emerge from the chrysalid state in July and lay their eggs on the leaves. To prevent an attack, spray with tar-oil in January or with liquid derris just before the blossom opens.

RED SPIDER   See under Plum.

Diseases

BACTERIAL CANKER   The yellow varieties e.g. 'Amber Heart' and 'Governor Wood' are most resistant. The disease occurs as yellow circles on the leaves which curl up. The fungus will spread on to the stems causing them to die back. It is destructive so spray with Bordeaux mixture (1 lb copper sulphate and $\frac{3}{4}$ lb slaked lime to 6 gals of water) in November and again in March.

CANKER   See under Apple.

SILVER LEAF   See under Plum.

GOOSEBERRY

Pests

APHIS   See under Raspberry.

SAWFLY   The most troublesome gooseberry pest, attacking the flower buds in spring and the open blossoms where it lays its eggs, the grubs falling to the ground late in June, to winter in the soil. The blossom bears no fruit. As routine, spray with Lindex when the blossom opens or with liquid derris.

Diseases

GREY MOULD (BOTRYTIS)   See also under Strawberries. With gooseberries, it attacks the new shoots and leaves causing them to die back which is its other name. It is most prevalent in a wet season or where the plants have grown 'soft' with too much nitrogen in the soil. To prevent, dust with Orthocide as the flowers open.

LEAF SPOT   This often appears after a wet season, or where the soil is waterlogged, as brown spots on the leaves, causing them to fall prematurely. To control, spray with Bordeaux mixture after gathering the fruit.

PEACH

Pests
APHIS   See under Apple. Spray peaches with liquid derris in spring.

MEALY BUG   See under Vine.

RED SPIDER   See under Plum.

SCALE   The insects cluster on the stems like white scales where they suck the sap reducing the vitality of the plant. To prevent, spray with tar-oil in December or with malathion in early spring.

Diseases
BACTERIAL CANKER   See under Cherry.

LEAF CURL   The most troublesome of peach diseases, usually appearing in a wet year, the fungus attacking the leaves, causing the edges to curl before turning brown and dying, later spreading to the stems when the tree will lose vitality. To prevent, spray early in spring with a 2 per cent lime-sulphur solution.

PEAR

Pests
BLOSSOM WEEVIL   See under Apple.

CODLING MOTH   See under Apple.

LEAF BLISTER MIDGE   These attack the leaves and fruits causing reddish-brown blisters to appear, beneath which the eggs are laid. The mites are invisible to the eye and winter in the bud scales. To control, spray with 1 in 50 lime-sulphur in April, though not on 'Doyenne du Comice'.

PEAR MIDGE   Eggs are laid on the blossom early April (late flowering varieties seem to escape), the maggots tunnelling into the fruit. Afterwards they fall to the ground to pupate in the soil. Dust or spray the trees with derris in spring.

TORTRIX MOTH   See under Apple.

WINTER MOTH   See under Apple.

Diseases

CANKER   See under Apple.

SCAB   Biologically different from Apple Scab and each cannot affect the other. It affects the shoots as black blisters and later the fruits. To control, spray with Bordeaux mixture at bud burst.

PLUM

Pests

RED SPIDER   This also attacks damsons and peaches, particularly where growing against a wall. The red insects with spider-like legs cluster on the underside of the leaves sucking the sap. To control, spray plums and damsons with DNOC in the dormant stage; peaches and apricots with malathion.

SAWFLY   This mostly attacks plums and gooseberries when in bloom, feeding on the pollen and here the eggs are laid, also in holes made in the buds. To prevent, spray with Lindex in spring or with liquid derris mixed with a spreader.

Diseases

BROWN ROT   See under Apple.

CANKER   See under Apple.

CLUSTER CUP   This occurs on the underside of the leaves as clusters of orange cups with small black dots on the upper surface. There is no cure.

SILVER LEAF   Most serious of plum and cherry diseases, the foliage turning a silver colour and soon the tree will die back entirely. The two most prolific croppers, 'Czar' and 'Victoria' are the most susceptible. Pruning is done only between March and July 15th, to allow the trees time to 'gum' and close up the wounds which they will not do in winter. If branches break treat with white lead paint.

100

RASPBERRY

Pests

APHIS   The insects penetrate the stems causing virus diseases to enter. Their presence is noted by swellings on the canes. A tar-oil wash in January will give control, or spray with liquid derris in April before the fruit sets.

RASPBERRY BEETLE   The most troublesome of raspberry pests, the tiny grey beetle lays her eggs in the flowers, the white grubs later feeding on the fruits and remaining on them after picking. They are always present and as routine, dust the flowers with derris as they open and again when the fruit begins to set.

RASPBERRY MOTH   This winters in the soil at the base of the canes, emerging from a cocoon in spring as a silvery-brown moth. It lays in the blossom like the Beetle, the grubs feeding on the fruits. To prevent, soak the soil around the canes with tar-oil in January and dust the blossom with derris as it opens.

Diseases

CANE BLIGHT   Similar to Cane Spot, but it attacks the canes at soil level causing them to wilt and die. There is no specific cure but spraying with Bordeaux mixture is helpful.

CANE SPOT   A fungus which attacks young canes showing as purple markings in summer, causing the canes to die back to the infected part. To prevent, spray with Bordeaux mixture in April at leaf burst.

MOSAIC   A virus disease possibly introduced by aphis and present in the sap causing the leaves to turn yellow. If noticed, pull up infected canes for there is no cure. If experienced, plant virus-resistant varieties.

RED CURRANT

Pest

CLEARWING MOTH   This lays its eggs along the branches and upon hatching, the grubs penetrate the stems causing them to die back. Routine spraying in winter with tar-oil will prevent an outbreak.

STRAWBERRY

Pests

APHIS   The most troublesome of strawberry pests, feeding on the sap and reducing the vitality of the plant whilst providing an entry for virus diseases. Their presence is denoted by the curled leaves. To prevent, spray with Lindex or liquid derris in spring when the leaves have formed but before the blossom opens.

BLOSSOM WEEVIL   These lay their eggs in the blossom, feeding on the pollen and causing the flowers to be unfruitful. To prevent, dust the flower trusses with derris powder when opening and again 14 days later.

TARSONEMID MITE   The mites begin to lay their eggs in the heart of the plants when the new leaves unfold in spring. Dusting with flowers of sulphur at this time will give some control, also against mildew; or spray with a 2 per cent lime-sulphur solution. This will also give some control against red spider. Well drained soil in good heart will usually prevent the plants being troubled by pests or diseases.

Diseases

BOTRYTIS (MILDEW)   Both are forms of mildew, appearing as a powdery mould on the foliage, later on the fruits causing them to turn brown and decay. Dusting with flowers of sulphur gives some control but better control is given by 10 per cent Captan as in Orthocide dust and where used in spring (just before the flowers open) in damp, humid districts, up to 50 per cent of the crop can be saved. Here, plant resistant varieties such as 'Cambridge Early Pine' and 'Favourite'.

Index